Easy Learning Javascript

(2 Edition)

YANG HU

The complexity of life, because they do not understand to simplify the complex, simple is the beginning of wisdom. From the essence of practice, this book briefly explain the concept and vividly cultivate programming interest. You will learn it easy and fast.

http://en.verejava.com

Copyright © 2020 Yang Hu

All rights reserved.

ISBN: 9798634864228

CONTENTS

1. Javascript Basic Concept 3
   1.1 Javascript HelloWorld 3
   1.2 Variable 4
   1.3 Variable and Type 5
2. Operational Operator 7
   2.1 Arithmetic Operator 7
   2.2 Function 8
   2.3 Class 11
   2.4 Type Conversion 13
   2.5 DOM 14
   2.6 Event 17
   2.7 Create a Web Caculator 18
   2.8 Assignment Operator 21
   2.9 Relational Operator 23
   2.10 If Conditional Statement 24
   2.11 Logic Operator 26
3. Control Statement 30
   3.1 Switch Statement 30
   3.2 While Loop Statement 32
   3.3 For Loop Statement 33
4. Array 36
   4.1 One-Dimensional Array 36
   4.2 Select All Check Box 39
   4.3 Two-Dimensional Array 40
   4.4 Find Dog Game 41
   4.5 Secondary Linkage Drop-down 47
5. More Event 53
   5.1 Login Web Page 53
   5.2 MouseOver Thumbnail to Larger 55
6. CSS 56
   6.1 CSS Inside Tag Style 56
   6.2 CSS Inline Style 57

6.3 CSS Import Style 58
6.4 Class Reference Style 59
6.5 ID Reference Style 60
6.6 CSS Font Style 61
6.7 CSS_Background_Style 63
6.8 CSS Border Style 64
6.9 CSS Spacing Style 65
6.10 CSS Inner and Outer Margins 67
6.11 CSS List Style 69
6.12 CSS Float 70
6.13 CSS Position Style 72
6.14 CSS Visibility Style 75
6.15 CSS Association Style 77
6.16 CSS Hyperlink Style 80
6.17 CSS Union Style 81
7. DOM and Element Hierarchy 82
  7.1 Element Hierarchy...82
  7.2 Create Text Node 88
  7.3 Delete Node 92
  7.4 Replace Node 94
  7.5 Add Contact Example 96
  7.6 CSS Style Font 98
  7.7 CSS Change Class Selector 99
  7.8 CSS Overflow Expand and Close 101
  7.9 CSS Floating Highlighting 103
  7.10 Table Create Rows Columns 104
  7.11 Delete Table Row Column 107
8. Timer 109

Javascript HelloWorld

Javascript is a web page dynamic interactive language that used in web development.

1. Create a helloworld.html file with Notepad and open it in your browser to see the webpage

<html>: tag tells the browser that this is an HTML document.
<head>: tag is a container for metadata about content and charset.
<title>: tag defines the title of the document.
<body>: tag defines the document's body.
<script>: tag is used to define a client-side script (JavaScript).
document.write(): writes HTML content to document in browser

```html
<html>
<head>
<meta http-equiv="Content-Type" content="text/html; charset=UTF-8">
<title>First Web Page</title>
</head>
  <body>
    <script type="text/javascript">
        document.write("HelloWorld");
    </script>
  </body>
</html>
```

Result:

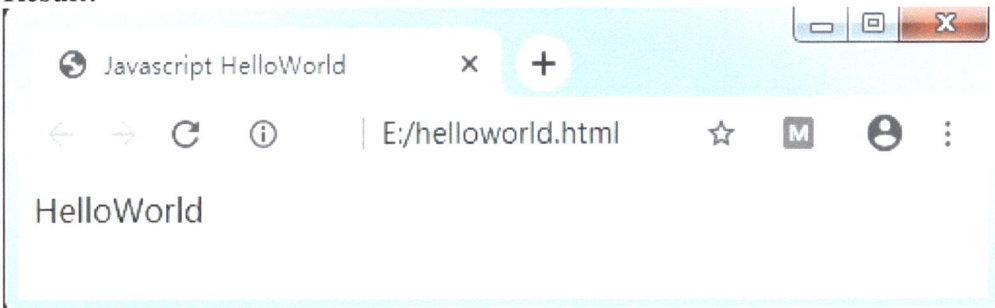

Variable

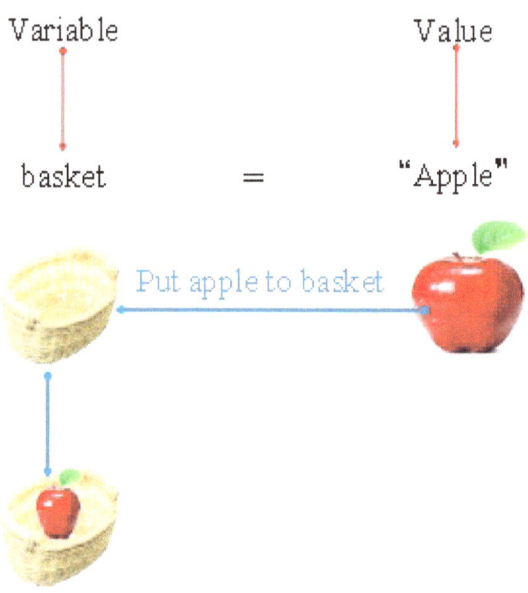

1. Create a file : Variable.html and open it in your browser

// : single comments are not executed by javascript
"": string type

```
<script type="text/javascript">
   var basket = "Apple";
   document.write(basket);
</script>
```

Result:

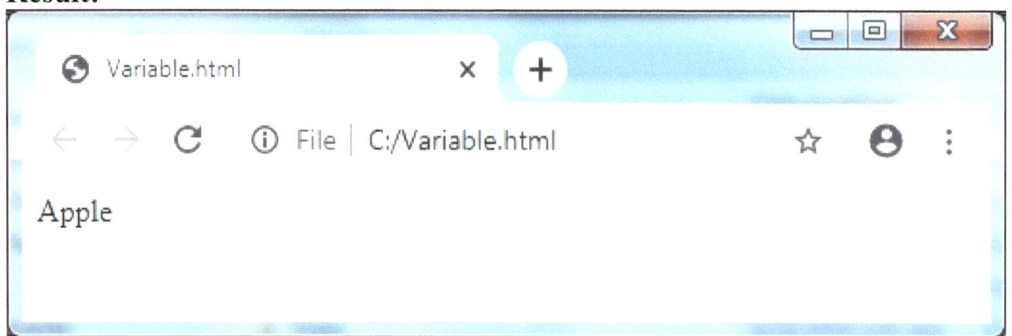

2.Change file : Variable.html Put "orange" **to replace** "apple".

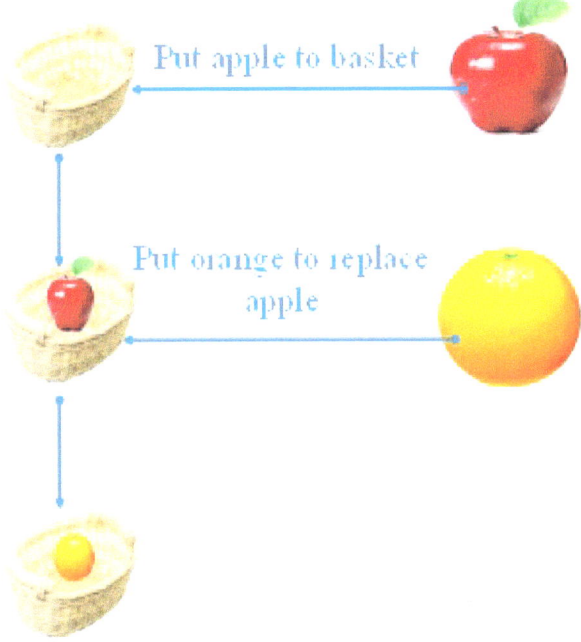

**
**: html tag wrap a new line

```
<script type="text/javascript">
   var basket = "Apple";
   document.write(basket);

   document.write("<br>");

   basket = "Orange";
   document.write(basket);
</script>
```

Run Result:

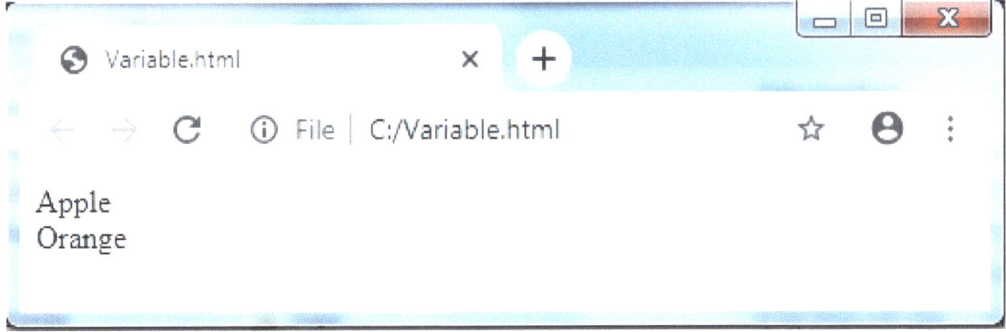

Variable and Type

Javascript is dynamic type language

1. Create a var.html **file with** Notepad **and open it in your browser to see the webpage**

typeof(): find the type of a JavaScript variable

```javascript
<script type="text/javascript">
   var x;           //undefined
   var a=9;         //number
   var b=1.5;       //number
   var c=true;      //Boolean
   var d="abc";     //string
   var e='abc';     //string

   document.write(typeof(x) + "<br>");
   document.write(typeof(a) + "<br>");
   document.write(typeof(b) + "<br>");
   document.write(typeof(c) + "<br>");
   document.write(typeof(d) + "<br>");
   document.write(typeof(e) + "<br>");
</script>
```

Result:

undefined
number
number
boolean
string
string

Arithmetic Operator

1. Create a *ArithmeticOperator.html* file with *Notepad* and open it in your browser
Arithmetic Operator:
   Add +, minus -, multiply *, divisible /, take modulo %

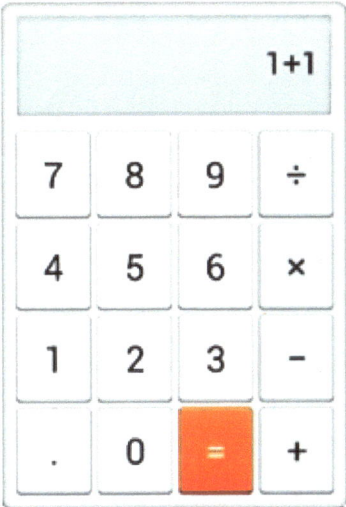

```
<script type="text/javascript">
   var a = 1;
   var b = 2;
   var c = 3;
   var d = 4;
   document.write(a + b); // = 3
   document.write("<br>");

   document.write(a - b); // = -1
   document.write("<br>");

   document.write(a * b); // = 2
   document.write("<br>");

   document.write(b / a); // = 2
   document.write("<br>");

   document.write(c % b); // = 1 //number remaining after divide
   document.write("<br>");
</script>
```

Function

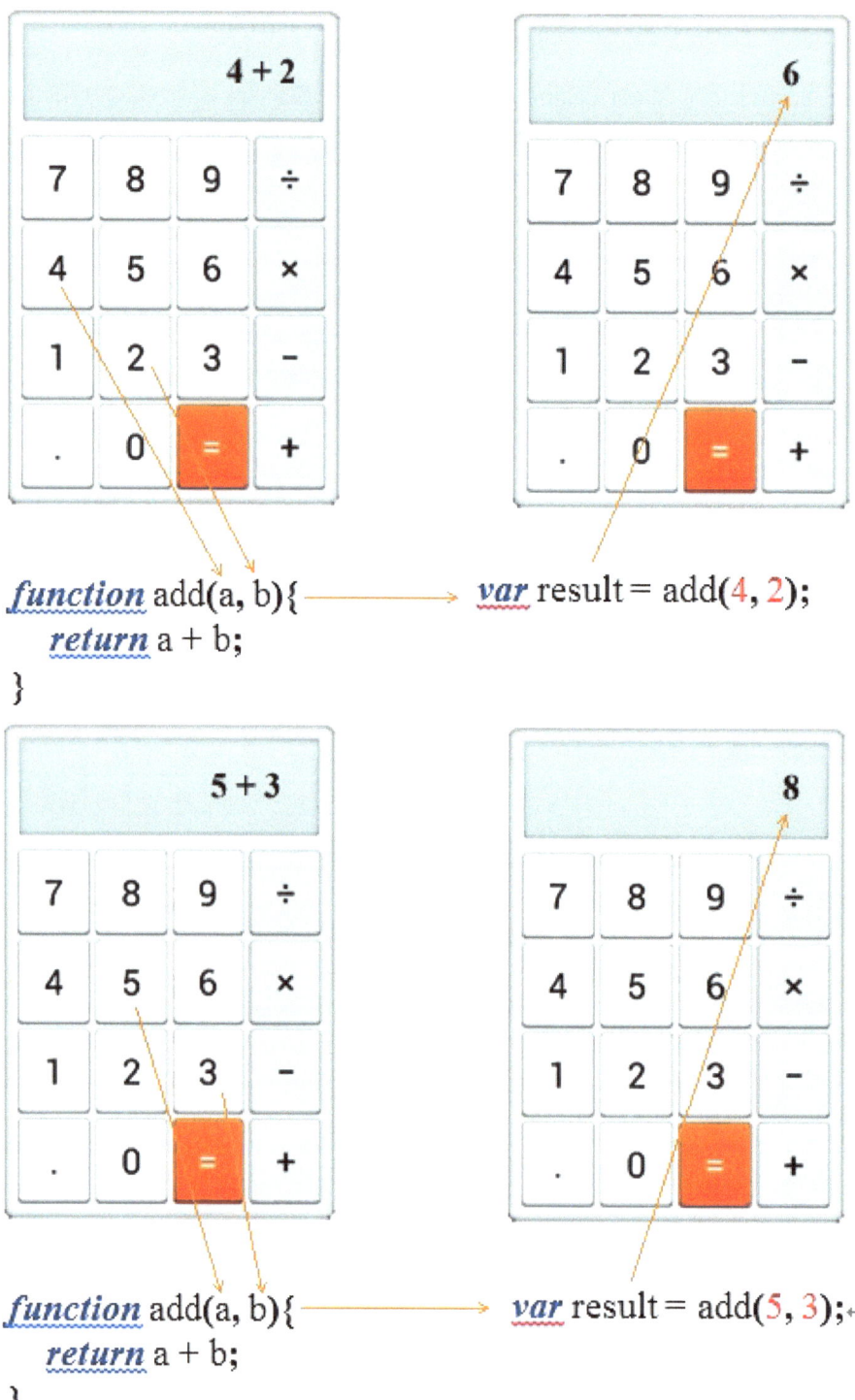

```
function add(a, b){        var result = add(5, 3);
    return a + b;
}
```
- Function Name: `add`
- Parameter: `(a, b)`
- Return Value: `var result = add(5, 3);`

1.Create a file : Function.html

```html
<script type="text/javascript">
  function add(a, b){
      return a + b;
  }

  var result = add(4, 2);
  document.write(result); // 6

  document.write("<br>");

  var result = add(5, 3);
  document.write(result)  // 8
</script>
```

Run Result:

6
8

2. Add 3 more functions about - , *, / to Function.html

```html
<script type="text/javascript">
  function add(a, b){
     return a + b;
  }

  function sub(a, b){
     return a - b;
  }

  function multiply(a, b){
     return a * b;
  }

  function divide(a, b){
     return a / b;
  }

  var result = add(4, 2);
  document.write(result); // 6

  document.write("<br>");

  var result = sub(4, 2);
  document.write(result)  // 2

  document.write("<br>");

  var result = multiply(4, 2);
  document.write(result)  // 8

  document.write("<br>");

  var result = divide(4, 2);
  document.write(result)  // 2

</script>
```

Class

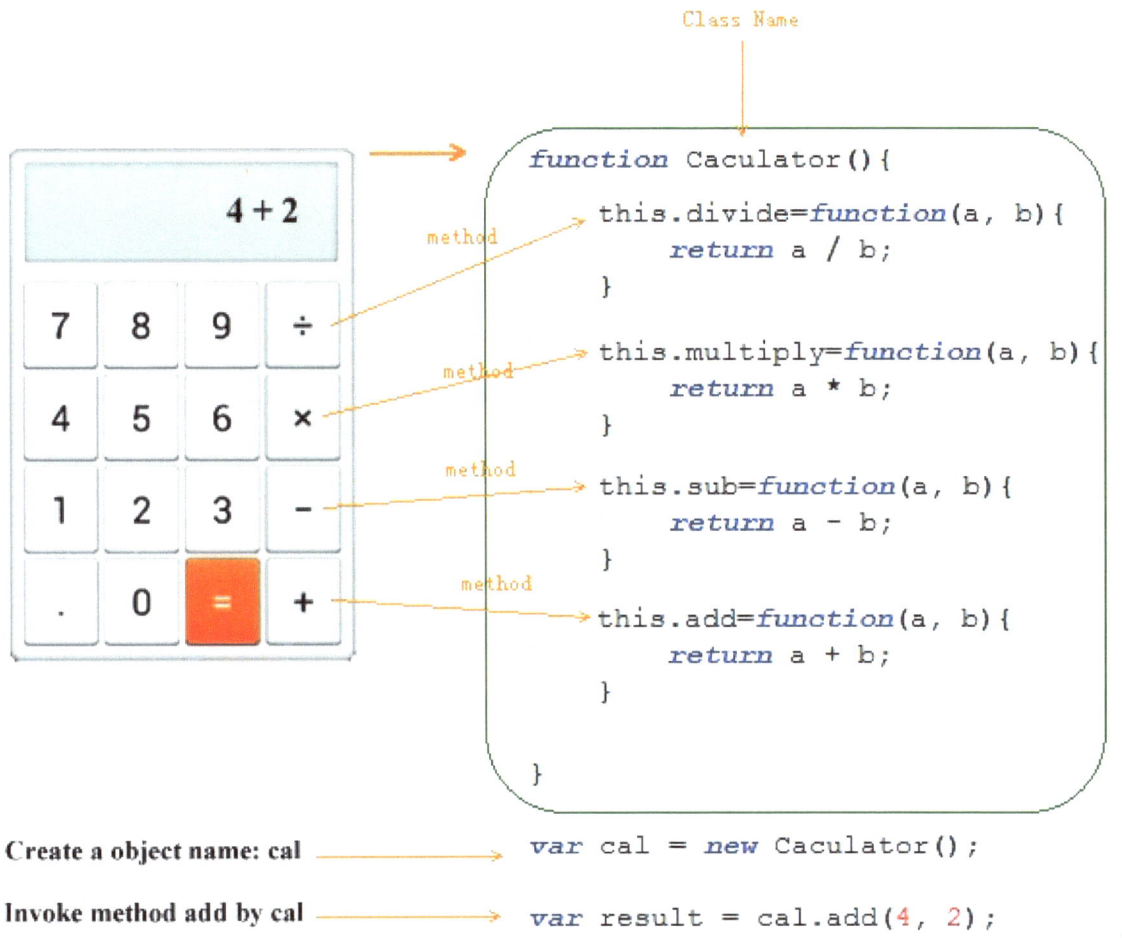

1.Create a file : Caculator.html

```html
<script type="text/javascript">

  function Caculator(){

    this.add=function(a, b){
       return a + b;
    }

    this.sub=function(a, b){
       return a - b;
    }

    this.multiply=function(a, b){
       return a * b;
    }

    this.divide=function(a, b){
       return a / b;
    }
  }

  var cal = new Caculator();

  var result = cal.add(4, 2);
  document.write(result); // 6

  var result = cal.sub(4, 2);
  document.write(result)  // 2

  var result = cal.multiply(4, 2);
  document.write(result)  // 8

  var result = cal.divide(4, 2);
  document.write(result)  // 2

</script>
```

Type Conversion

1. Create a TypeConversion.html

parseInt(): this is javascript default function can convert string to integer.

```html
<script type="text/javascript">
    var a="1";
    var b="2";

    var result = a + b; // + concatenate two strings
    document.write(result); // = 12

    document.write("<br>");

    result = parseInt(a) + parseInt(b);
    document.write(result); // = 3
</script>
```

Result:

12
3

DOM

DOM: In Javascript every HTML element is a class object.

Document Object Model structure diagram:

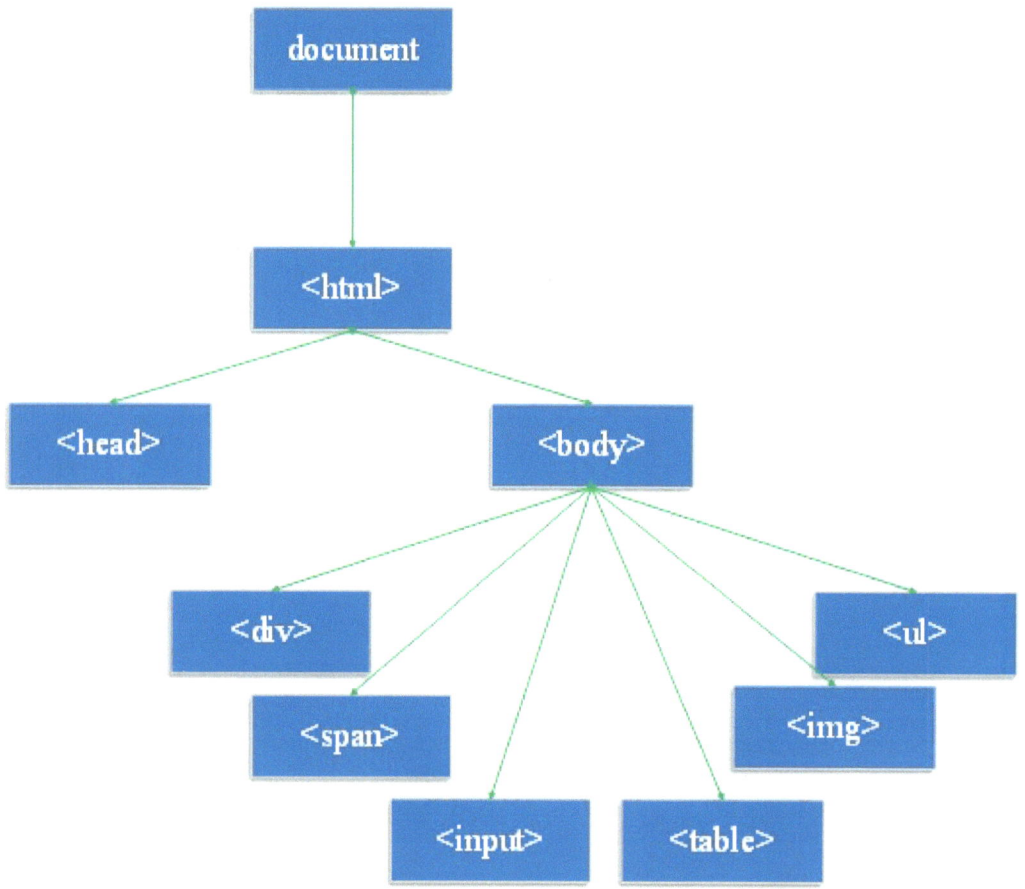

1.Create a file : getElementById.html

document.getElementById(): is a DOM method to get the element by ID attribute.
alert(): is a function to open a information window.
Obj.innerHTML: sets or returns the inner HTML content of an element.
<div>: tag defines a division or a section in an HTML document.

```html
<div id="word">Faith and Hope</div>

<script type="text/javascript">
   var divObj = document.getElementById("word");
   var htmlContent = divObj.innerHTML;
   alert(htmlContent);
</script>
```

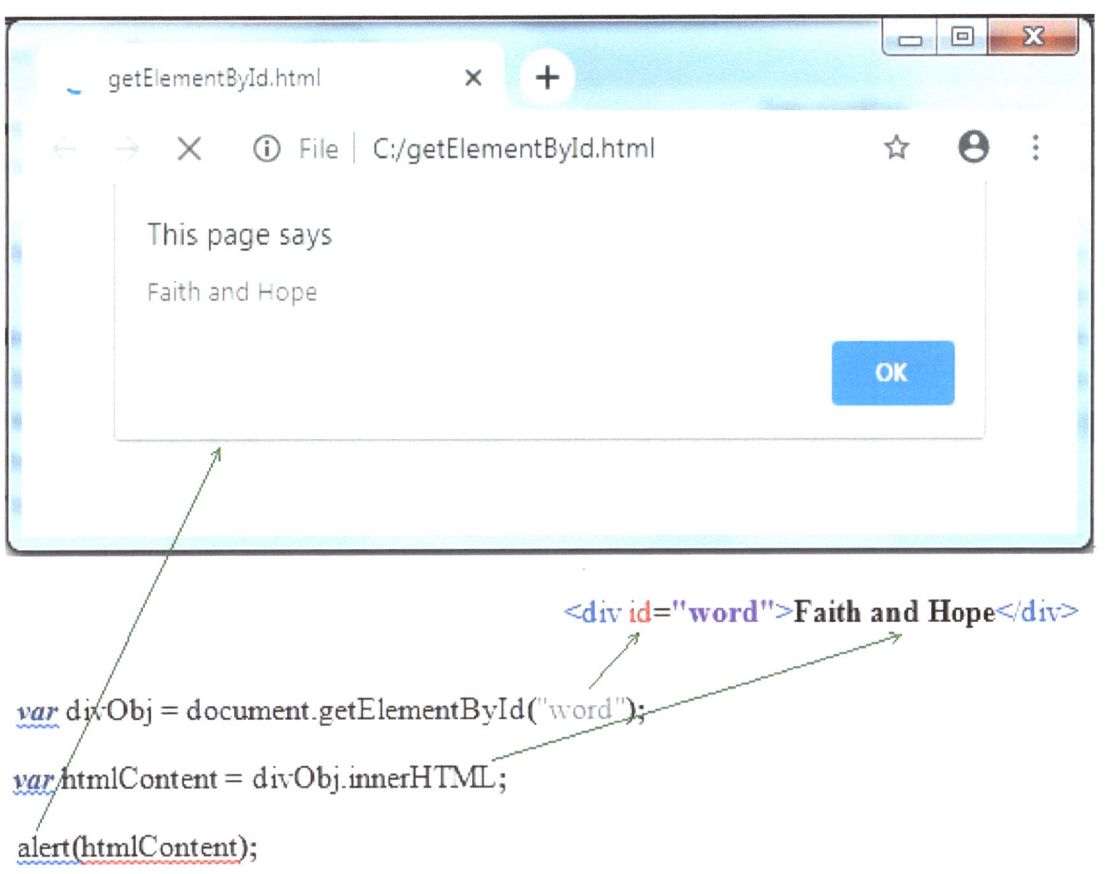

2. Change a file : getElementById.html

<input type="text" />: html tag specifies an input field where the user can enter data.

```
<input type="text" id="username" value="Joseph" />

<script type="text/javascript">
   var divObj = document.getElementById("username");
   var value = divObj.value;
   alert(value);
</script>
```

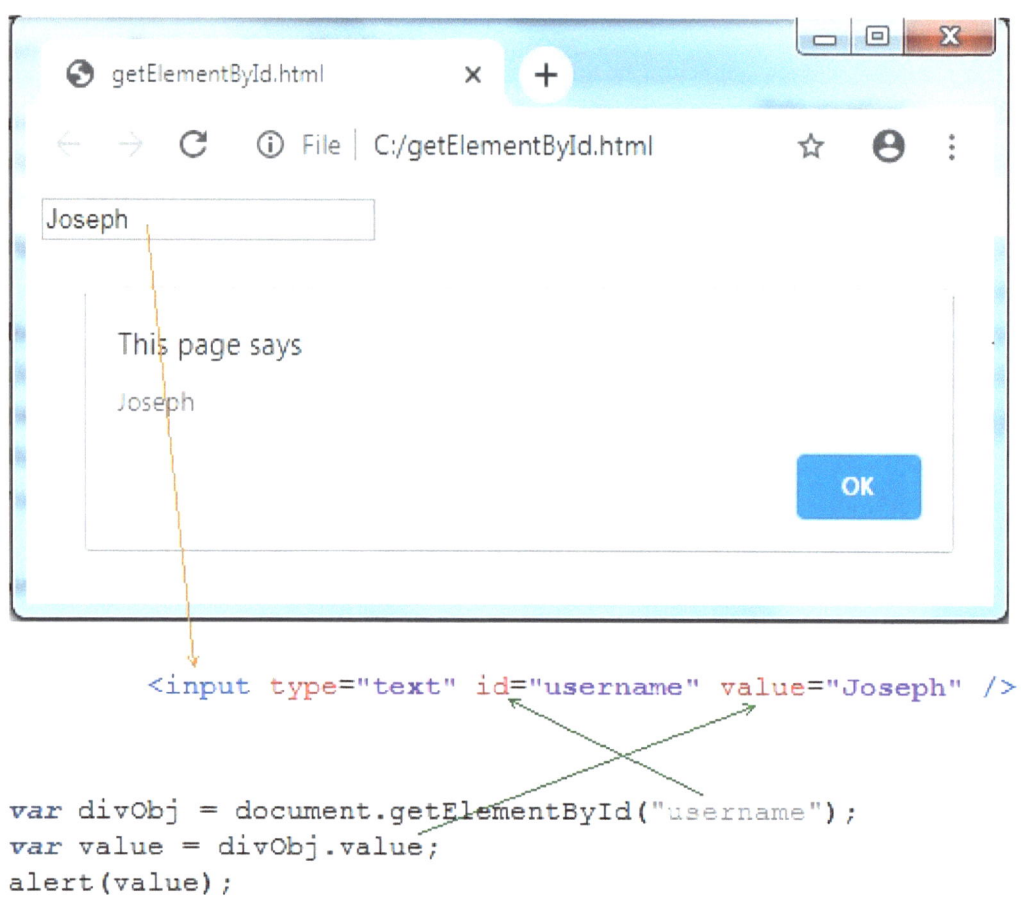

Event

1. Create a file : onClick.html

onClick: when the mouse clicks the button will call a function.
<input type="button" />: html tag defines a clickable button.

```html
<input type="text" id="username" value="Joseph" />
<input type="button" value="Click Me" onClick="doClick()" />

<script type="text/javascript">
  function doClick(){
    var divObj = document.getElementById("username");
    var value = divObj.value;
    alert(value);
  }
</script>
```

Create a Web Caculator

1.Create a file : WebCaculator.html

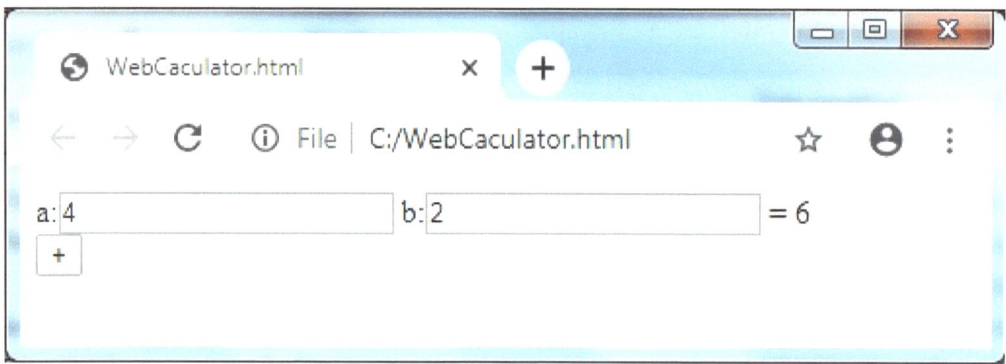

```
a:<input type="text" id="a" value="" />
b:<input type="text" id="b" value="" />
=
<span id="result"></span>
<br>
<input type="button" value="+" onClick="doAdd()" />

<script type="text/javascript">
  function doAdd(){
    var aObj = document.getElementById("a");
    var bObj = document.getElementById("b");
    var resultObj = document.getElementById("result");
    var a = parseInt(aObj.value); // Convert string to integer
    var b = parseInt(bObj.value);
    resultObj.innerHTML = a + b;
  }
</script>
```

2. Add 3 mores function - , * , / to WebCaculator.html

```html
a:<input type="text" id="a" value="" />
b:<input type="text" id="b" value="" />
=
<span id="result"></span>
<br>
<input type="button" value="+" onClick="doAdd()" />
<input type="button" value="-" onClick="doSub()" />
<input type="button" value="*" onClick="doMultiply()" />
<input type="button" value="/" onClick="doDivide()" />

<script type="text/javascript">
    function doAdd(){
        var aObj = document.getElementById("a");
        var bObj = document.getElementById("b");
        var resultObj = document.getElementById("result");
        var a = parseInt(aObj.value); // Convert string to integer
        var b = parseInt(bObj.value);
        resultObj.innerHTML = a + b;
    }

    function doSub(){
        var aObj = document.getElementById("a");
        var bObj = document.getElementById("b");
        var resultObj = document.getElementById("result");
        var a = parseInt(aObj.value); // Convert string to integer
        var b = parseInt(bObj.value);
        resultObj.innerHTML = a - b;
    }

    function doMultiply(){
        var aObj = document.getElementById("a");
        var bObj = document.getElementById("b");
        var resultObj = document.getElementById("result");
        var a = parseInt(aObj.value); // Convert string to integer
        var b = parseInt(bObj.value);
        resultObj.innerHTML = a * b;
    }
```

```
function doDivide(){
   var aObj = document.getElementById("a");
   var bObj = document.getElementById("b");
   var resultObj = document.getElementById("result");
   var a = parseInt(aObj.value); // Convert string to integer
   var b = parseInt(bObj.value);
   resultObj.innerHTML = a / b;
}
</script>
```

Click + button Result:

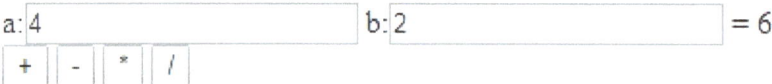

Click - button Result:

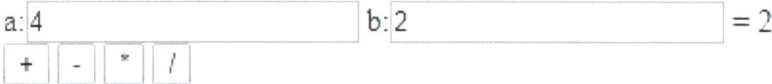

Click * button Result:

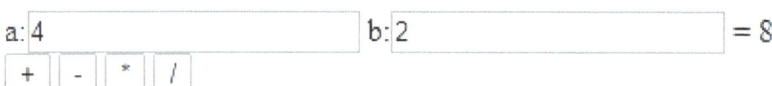

Click / button Result:

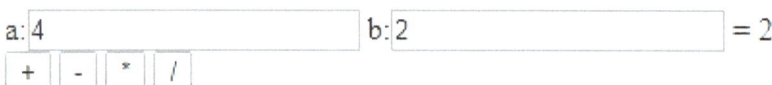

Assignment Operator

1. Create a AssignmentOperator.html file with Notepad and open it in your browser

```html
<script type="text/javascript">
  var d = 4;
  document.write(d++); // = 4 print d and then increment 1
  document.write("<br>");

  d = 4;
  document.write(++d); // = 5 increment 1 and then print d
  document.write("<br>");

  d = 4;
  document.write(d--); // = 4 print d and then decrement 1
  document.write("<br>");

  d = 4;
  document.write(--d); // = 3 decrement 1 and then print d

  var result = 10;
  result = result + 1;
  document.write(result); // = 11
  document.write("<br>");

  result = 10;
  result++;
  document.write(result); // = 11
  document.write("<br>");

  result = 10;
  result += 1;
  document.write(result);  // = 11
  document.write("<br>");
</script>
```

2. Create a quantity adder and subtracter quantity.html

Click + button to increase the quantity by 1, and click - button to decrease the quantity by 1.

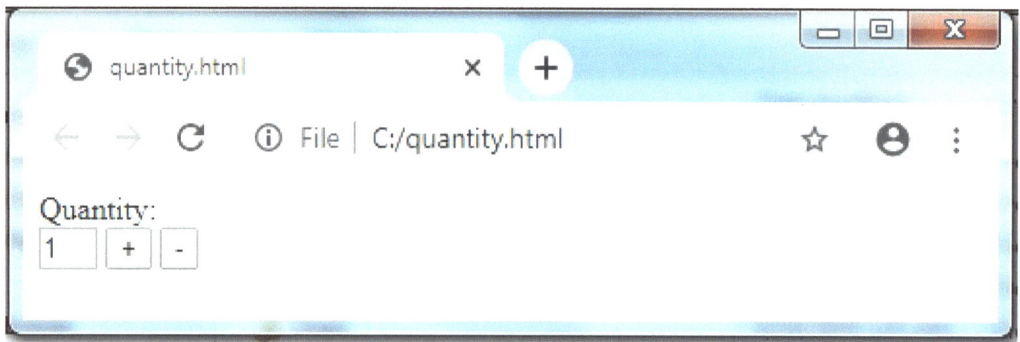

Quantity:
```
<br>
<input type="text" style="width:30px" id="quantity" value="1" />
<input type="button" value="+" onClick="doAdd()" />
<input type="button" value="-" onClick="doSub()" />

<script type="text/javascript">
  function doAdd(){
    var quantityObj = document.getElementById("quantity");
    var value = parseInt(quantityObj.value);
    value++
    quantityObj.value = value;
  }

  function doSub(){
    var quantityObj = document.getElementById("quantity");
    var value = parseInt(quantityObj.value);
    value--
    quantityObj.value = value;
  }
</script>
```

Relational Operator

1. Create a RelationalOperator.html file with Notepad and open it in your browser

Relational operators only two value: true, false

```html
<script type="text/javascript">

    document.write(1 > 2); // false
    document.write("<br>");

    document.write(1 >= 1); // true
    document.write("<br>");

    document.write(1 < 2); // true
    document.write("<br>");

    document.write(1 <= 2); // true
    document.write("<br>");

    document.write(1 == 1); // true
    document.write("<br>");

    document.write(1 != 2); // true

</script>
```

If Conditional Statement

If statement
1. if(expression){statement}
2. if (expression) { statement } else { statement }
3. if (expression) {statement } else if { statement }

1. Create a If.html file with Notepad and open it in your browser

Score example:
if score == 5 : Excellent
else if score == 4:   Good
else: Need to catch up

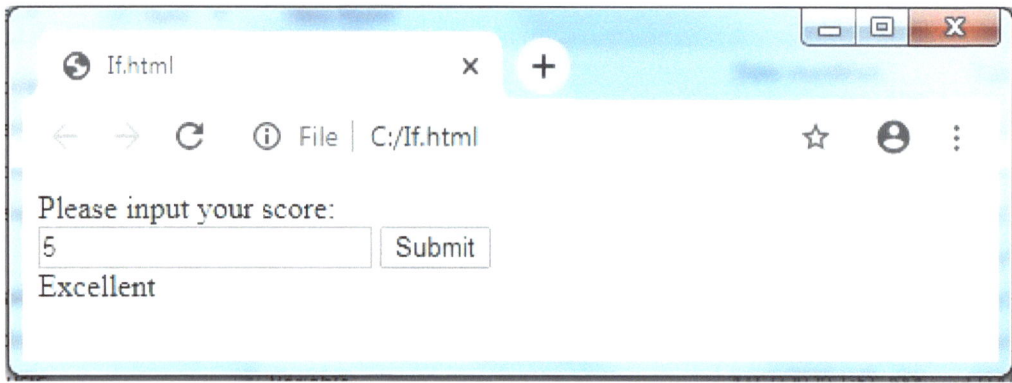

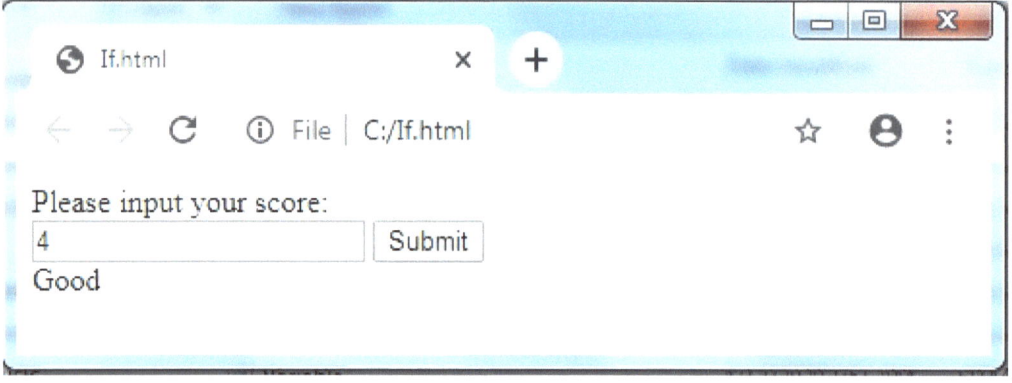

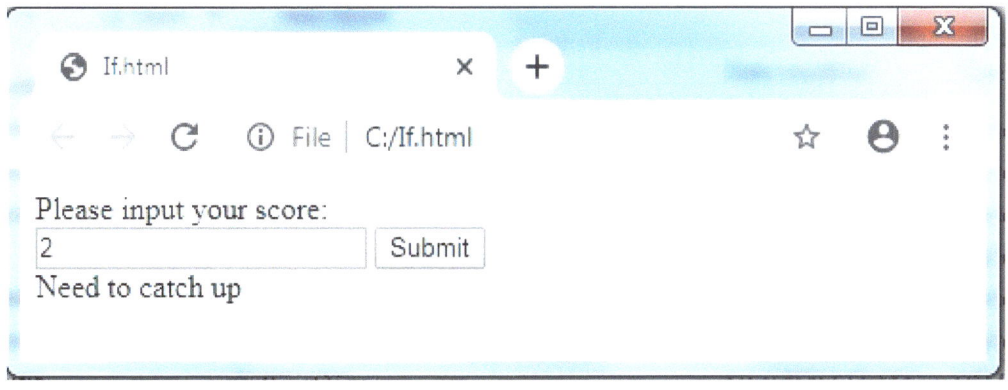

Please input your score:
\<br\>
\<input type=**"text"** id=**"score"** value=**""** /\>
\<input type=**"button"** value=**"Submit"** onClick=**"doSubmit()"** /\>
\<br\>
\<span id=**"message"**\>\</span\>

\<script type=**"text/javascript"**\>
  function doSubmit(){
    var scoreObj = document.getElementById("score");
    var messageObj = document.getElementById("message");

    var score = parseInt(scoreObj.value);
    if (score == 5) {
      messageObj.innerHTML = "Excellent";
    } *else if* (score == 4) {
      messageObj.innerHTML = "Good";
    } *else* {
      messageObj.innerHTML = "Need to catch up";
    }
  }
\</script\>

Logic Operator

1. Create a LogicOperator.html file with Notepad and open it in your browser

Logical Operator: and &&, or ||, not !
   1. && returns true if both sides of the operation are true, otherwise false
   2. || The result is false when both sides of the operation are false, otherwise true;
   3. ! if returns true, the result is false, otherwise is true

```html
<script type="text/javascript">
    document.write(true && false); // false
    document.write("<br>");

    document.write(false && true); // false
    document.write("<br>");

    document.write(false && false); // false
    document.write("<br>");

    document.write(true && true); // true
    document.write("<br>");

    document.write(true || false); // true
    document.write("<br>");

    document.write(false || true); // true
    document.write("<br>");

    document.write(true || true); // true
    document.write("<br>");

    document.write(false || false); // false
    document.write("<br>");

    document.write(!true); // false
    document.write("<br>");

    document.write(!false); // true
    document.write("<br>");
</script>
```

2. Create a LogicOperator2.html

```html
<script type="text/javascript">

    document.write(1>2 && 3>4) // = false
    document.write(2>1 && 3>4) // = false

    document.write("-------------")

    document.write(2>1 || 3>4) // = true
    document.write(2>1 || 3>4) // = true
    document.write(1>2 || 3>4) // = false

</script>
```

3. Payroll tax example:
Tax amount = salary * tax rate
level:
500 -- 2000 $: tax rate 10%
2000--5000 $:   tax rate 15%
5000-- 20000 $: tax rate 20%
    More than 20000$:   tax rate 30%

```javascript
<script type="text/javascript">
   var salary = 10000;
   var tax = 0;
   if (salary >= 500 && salary < 2000) {
      tax = salary * 0.1;
   } else if (salary >= 2000 && salary < 5000) {
      tax = salary * 0.15;
   } else if (salary >= 5000 && salary < 20000) {
      tax = salary * 0.2;
   } else {
      tax = salary * 0.3;
   }
   document.write("tax amount=" + tax);
</script>
```

Result:

tax amount=2000

2. Create a WebTax.html

Input salary and then click Calculate Tax button

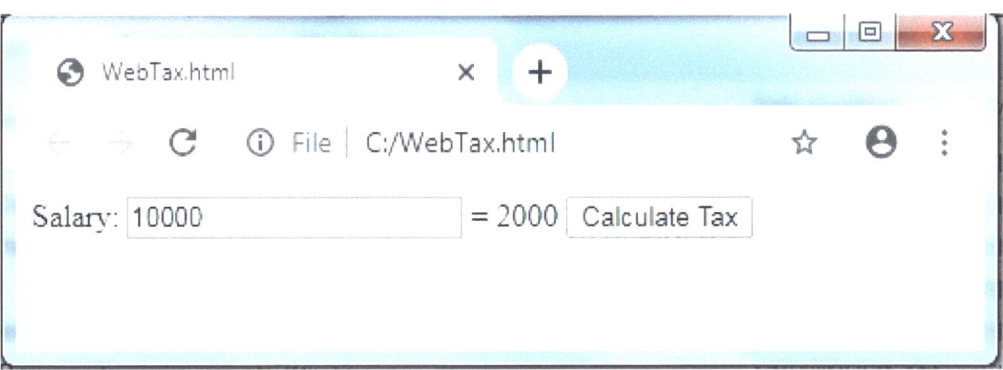

```
Salary: <input type="text" id="salary" value="" />
=
<span id="tax"></span>
<input type="button" value="Calculate Tax" onClick="doTax()" />

<script type="text/javascript">

  function doTax(){
     var salaryObj = document.getElementById("salary");
     var salary = parseInt(salaryObj.value);
     var tax = 0;
     if (salary >= 500 && salary < 2000) {
        tax = salary * 0.1;
     } else if (salary >= 2000 && salary < 5000) {
        tax = salary * 0.15;
     } else if (salary >= 5000 && salary < 20000) {
        tax = salary * 0.2;
     } else {
        tax = salary * 0.3;
     }
     document.getElementById("tax").innerHTML = tax;
  }

</script>
```

Switch Statement

1. Create a switch.html file with Notepad and open it in your browser

Input a number 1 , 2, 3
    1 : Pay by Visa Card
    2 : Pay by Master Card
    3: Pay by Paypal
       Otherwise Pay by face to face

```javascript
<script type="text/javascript">

   var num = 1;

   switch (num) {
      case 1:
         document.write("Pay by Visa Card");
         break; // terminate the code to continue execution
      case 2:
         document.write("Pay by Master Card");
         break;
      case 3:
         document.write("Pay by Paypal");
         break;
      default:
         document.write("Pay by face to face");
   }

</script>
```

Result:

Pay by Visa Card

2. Create a WebPay.html

this: current element object

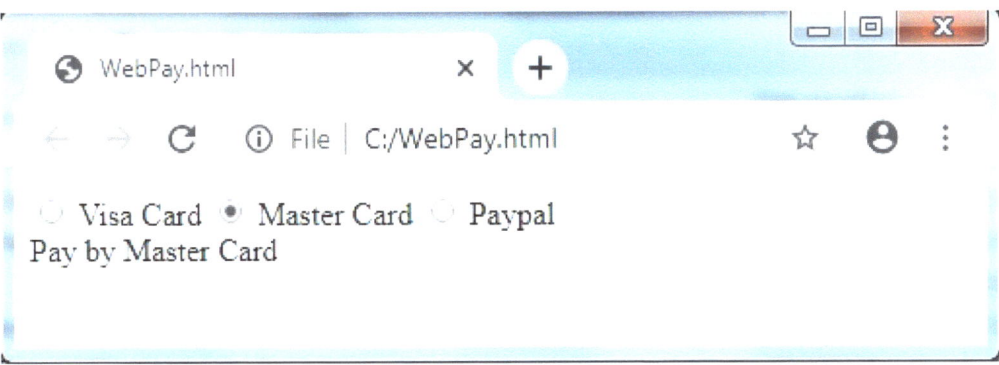

```html
<input type="radio" name="card" value="1" onclick="doPay(this)" /> Visa Card
<input type="radio" name="card" value="2" onclick="doPay(this)" /> Master Card
<input type="radio" name="card" value="3" onclick="doPay(this)" /> Paypal
<br>
<span id="result"></span>

<script type="text/javascript">

  function doPay(obj){
     var num = parseInt(obj.value);
     var resultObj = document.getElementById("result");

     switch (num) {
        case 1:
           resultObj.innerHTML = "Pay by Visa Card";
           break;
        case 2:
           resultObj.innerHTML = "Pay by Master Card";
           break;
        case 3:
           resultObj.innerHTML = "Pay by Paypal";
           break;
        default:
           resultObj.innerHTML = "Pay by face to face";
     }
  }
</script>
```

While Loop Statement

while(expression){
  statement;
}
continues execution if the expression is true, otherwise exits loop

```
var i = 0;
while (i < 10)            i=0 < 10 true executes the loop code
{
   document.write(i+".");  i=1
   i++;
}


while (i < 10)            i=1 < 10 true executes the loop code
{
   document.write(i+".");  i=2
   i++;
}


while (i < 10)            i=2 < 10 true executes the loop code
{
   document.write(i+".");
   i++;                    i=3
}
         Until i = 9

while (i < 10)            i=9 < 10 true executes the loop code
{
   document.write(i+".");  i=10
   i++;
}


while (i < 10)            i=10 < 10 False terminated
{
   document.write(i+".");  i=11
   i++;
}
```

* While Loop is terminated

1. Create a WhileLoop.html file with Notepad and open it in your browser

```
<script type="text/javascript">

   var i = 0;
   while (i < 10)
   {
      document.write(i+",");
      i++;
   }

</script>
```

Result:

0,1,2,3,4,5,6,7,8,9,

For Loop Statement

```
for (var i = 0; i < 10; i++) {
    document.write(i + ".");
}
```
i=0 < 10 true executes the loop code

i++

```
for (var i = 0; i < 10; i++) {
    document.write(i + ".");
}
```
i=1 < 10 true executes the loop code

i++

```
for (var i = 0; i < 10; i++) {
    document.write(i + ".");
}
```
i=2 < 10 true executes the loop code

i++

Until i = 9

```
for (var i = 0; i < 10; i++) {
    document.write(i + ".");
}
```
i=9 < 10 true executes the loop code

i++

```
for (var i = 0; i < 10; i++) {
    document.write(i + ".");
}
```
i=10 < 10 False terminated

i++

For Loop is terminated

1. Create a ForLoop.html file with Notepad and open it in your browser

```
<script type="text/javascript">

  for (var i = 0; i < 10; i++) {
     document.write(i + ",");
  }

</script>
```

Result:

0,1,2,3,4,5,6,7,8,9,

One-Dimensional Array

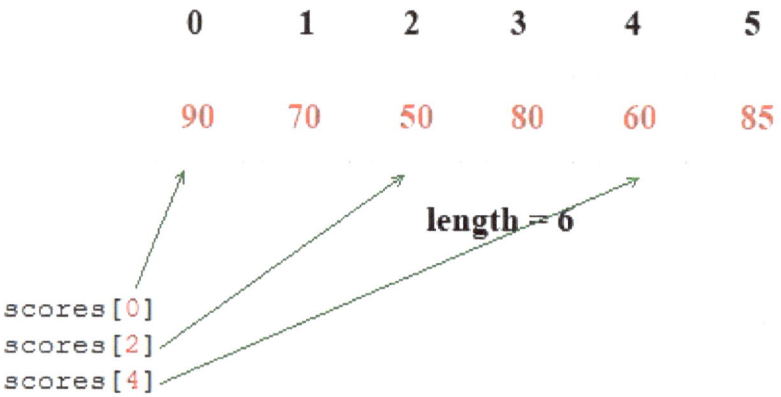

1. Create a OneArray.html file with Notepad and open it in your browser

```
<script type="text/javascript">

   // One-dimensional array definition and initialization
   var scores = [ 90, 70, 50, 80, 60, 85 ];

   document.write(scores[0] + "<br>");
   document.write(scores[2] + "<br>");
   document.write(scores[4] + "<br>");

</script>
```

Result:

90
50
60

2. Change OneArray.html print all scores of the array

Scores.length: the total count of array

```
<script type="text/javascript">

   var scores = [ 90, 70, 50, 80, 60, 85 ];

   //print all the scores of the array
   for (var i = 0; i < scores.length; i++) {
      document.write(scores[i] + ",");
   }

</script>
```

Result:

90,70,50,80,60,85,

3. Change OneArray.html print all scores of the array

```html
<script type="text/javascript">

  // Dynamically define a one-dimensional array
  var scores = new Array();
  scores[0] = 90;
  scores[1] = 70;
  scores[2] = 50;
  scores[3] = 80;
  scores[4] = 60;
  scores[5] = 85;

  //print all the scores of the array
  for (var i = 0; i < scores.length; i++) {
     document.write(scores[i] + ",");
  }

</script>
```

Result:

90,70,50,80,60,85,

Select All Check Box

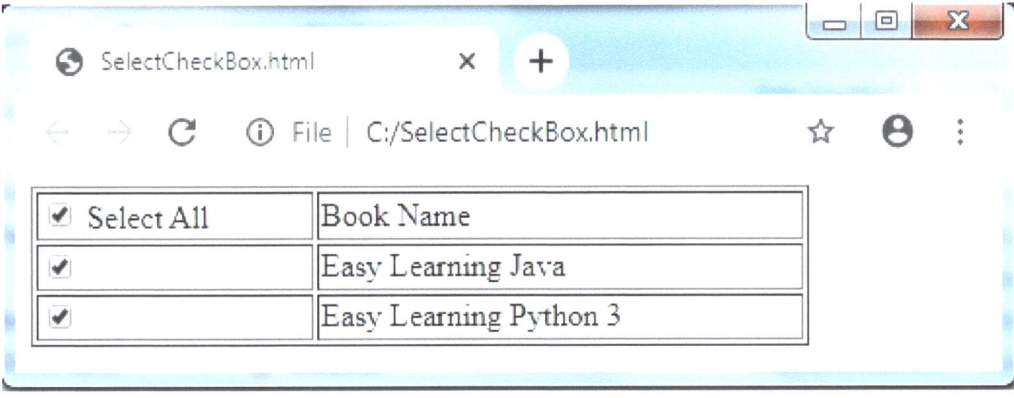

1. Create a SelectCheckBox.html **file with** Notepad **and open it in your browser**
document.getElementsByName(): get an array of elements with the same name
checked: if the checkbox is checked

```html
<table width="400" border="1">
  <tr>
    <td><input type="checkbox" onclick="checkAll(this)" /> Select All</td>
    <td>Book Name</td>
  </tr>
  <tr>
    <td><input type="checkbox" name="book" /></td>
    <td>Easy Learning Java</td>
  </tr>
  <tr>
    <td><input type="checkbox" name="book" /></td>
    <td>Easy Learning Python 3</td>
  </tr>
</table>
<script language="JavaScript">
  function checkAll(obj)
  {
    var bookArray=document.getElementsByName("book");
    for(var i=0;i<bookArray.length;i++)
    {
      bookArray[i].checked=obj.checked;
    }
  }
</script>
```

Two-Dimensional Array

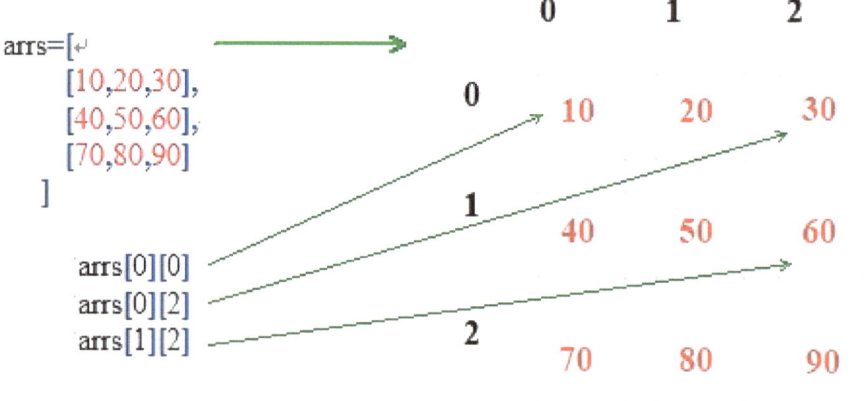

1. Create a TwoArray.html file with Notepad and open it in your browser

```html
<script type="text/javascript">

    // Two-dimensional array definition and initialization
    var arrs =[
       [ 10, 20, 30 ],
       [ 40, 50, 60 ],
       [ 70, 80, 90 ]
    ];

    document.write(arrs[0][0] + "<br>");
    document.write(arrs[0][2] + "<br>");
    document.write(arrs[1][2] + "<br>");

</script>
```

Result:

10
30
60

2. Create a TwoArray2.html file with Notepad and open it in your browser

i: row index, j: column index

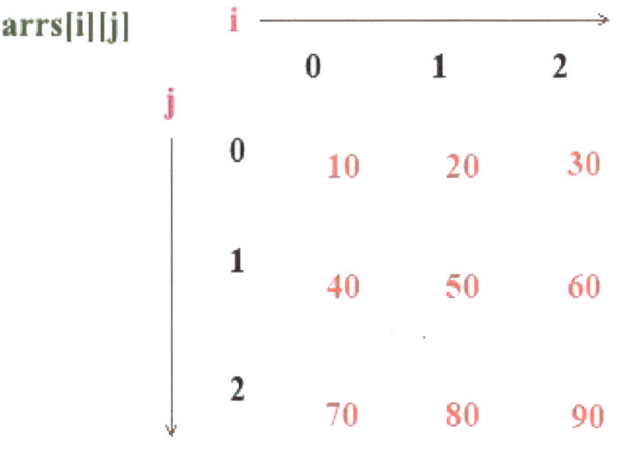

```
<script type="text/javascript">

  var arrs =[
    [ 10, 20, 30 ],
    [ 40, 50, 60 ],
    [ 70, 80, 90 ]
  ];

  // i: row index, j: column index
  for (var i = 0; i < arrs.length; i++) {
    for (var j = 0; j < arrs[i].length; j++) {
       document.write(arrs[i][j]);
       document.write(" ");
    }
    document.write("<br>");
  }

</script>
```

Find Dog Game

1. Draw buttons according to two-dimensional array maps

```
var maps =[
    [ 1, 1, 1, 1 ],
    [ 1, 1, 1, 1 ],
    [ 1, 2, 1, 1 ],
    [ 1, 1, 1, 1 ]
];
```

```html
<style>
  input{
     width:40px;
     height:40px;
  }
</style>

<span id="result"></span>

<script type="text/javascript">
  var maps =[
    [ 1, 1, 1, 1 ],
    [ 1, 1, 1, 1 ],
    [ 1, 2, 1, 1 ],
    [ 1, 1, 1, 1 ]
  ];
  var mapHTML = "";
  for (var i = 0; i < maps.length; i++) {
     for (var j = 0; j < maps[i].length; j++) {
        mapHTML +="<input type='button' value=' ' />";
     }
     mapHTML +="<br>";
  }
  document.getElementById("result").innerHTML = mapHTML;
</script>
```

2. Fill in the value of the array into the button, and add a button click event, if button value is 1 becomes *, if button value is 2 becomes Dog

```
                  1:  *
                  2:  Dog

 var maps =[
     [ 1, 1, 1, 1 ],
     [ 1, 1, 1, 1 ],
     [ 1, 2, 1, 1 ],
     [ 1, 1, 1, 1 ]
 ];
```

1:   *
2:   Dog

```
<style>
  input{
     width:40px;
     height:40px;
  }
</style>

<span id="result"></span>

<script type="text/javascript">
  var maps =[
     [ 1, 1, 1, 1 ],
     [ 1, 1, 1, 1 ],
     [ 1, 2, 1, 1 ],
     [ 1, 1, 1, 1 ]
  ];

  var mapHTML = "";
  for (var i = 0; i < maps.length; i++) {
     for (var j = 0; j < maps[i].length; j++) {
        mapHTML +="<input type='button' value=' ' onClick='doButtonClick(this,"+maps[i][j]+")' />";
     }
     mapHTML +="<br>";
  }
  document.getElementById("result").innerHTML = mapHTML;
```

```
function doButtonClick(obj,value){
    if(value == 1){
        obj.value = "*";
    }else if(value == 2){
        obj.value = "Dog";
    }
}
</script>
```

3. Print random numbers 0-9

Math.random(): returns a random number between 0 and 1.
Math.floor(): rounds a number downwards to the nearest integer

```
<script type="text/javascript">
    for(var i=0;i<10;i++){
        var num = Math.floor(Math.random() * 10)
        document.write(num + ", ");
    }
</script>
```

Result:

9, 3, 9, 0, 4, 1, 0, 3, 4, 5,

4. Randomly generate 1- 2 initialize two-dimensional array, Fill in the value of the array into the button, and add a button click event, if button value is 1 becomes *, if button value is 2 becomes Dog

1:   *
2:   Dog

```html
<style>
  input{
    width:40px;
    height:40px;
  }
</style>

<span id="result"></span>

<script type="text/javascript">
  var maps =[
    [ 0, 0, 0, 0 ],
    [ 0, 0, 0, 0 ],
    [ 0, 0, 0, 0 ],
    [ 0, 0, 0, 0 ]
  ];

  for (var i = 0; i < maps.length; i++) {
    for (var j = 0; j < maps[i].length; j++) {
      var num = Math.floor(Math.random()*2)+1;
      maps[i][j] = num;
    }
  }
```

```
var mapHTML = "";
for (var i = 0; i < maps.length; i++) {
    for (var j = 0; j < maps[i].length; j++) {
        mapHTML +="<input type='button' value=' ' onClick='doButtonClick(this,"+maps[i][j]+")' />";
    }
    mapHTML +="<br>";
}
document.getElementById("result").innerHTML = mapHTML;


function doButtonClick(obj,value){
    if(value == 1){
        obj.value = "*";
    }else if(value == 2){
        obj.value = "Dog";
    }
}
</script>
```

Secondary Linkage Drop-down

1. Create a Drop-down.html file with Notepad and open it in your browser

window.onload: execute a function after a page has been loaded
document.createElement(): create a html element

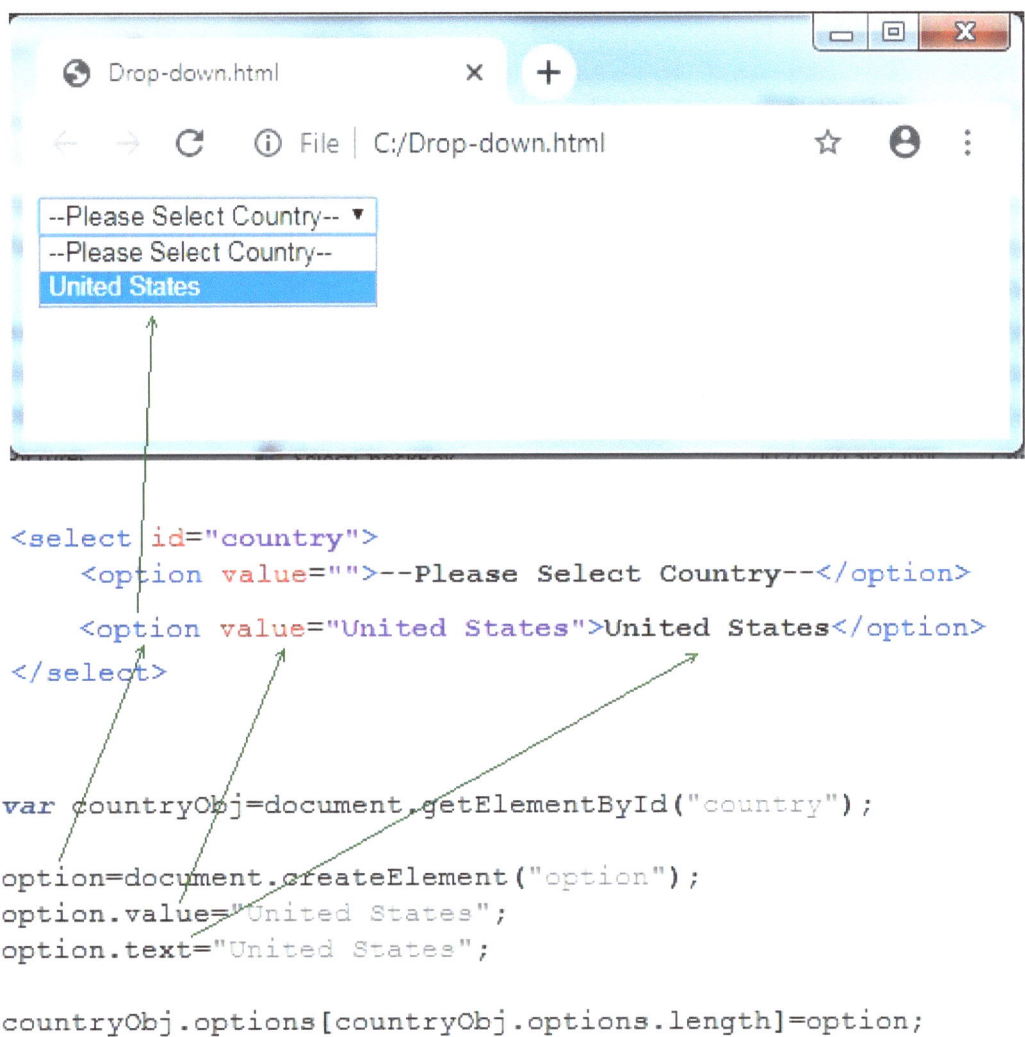

```
<select id="country">
    <option value="">--Please Select Country--</option>
    <option value="United States">United States</option>
</select>


var countryObj=document.getElementById("country");

option=document.createElement("option");
option.value="United States";
option.text="United States";

countryObj.options[countryObj.options.length]=option;
```

```html
<select id="country">
  <option value="">--Please Select Country--</option>
</select>

<script type="text/javascript">

  window.onload=function()
  {
    var countryObj=document.getElementById("country");

    option=document.createElement("option");
    option.text="United States";
    option.value="United States";

    countryObj.options[countryObj.options.length]=option;
  }

</script>
```

2. Add more options by countryArray

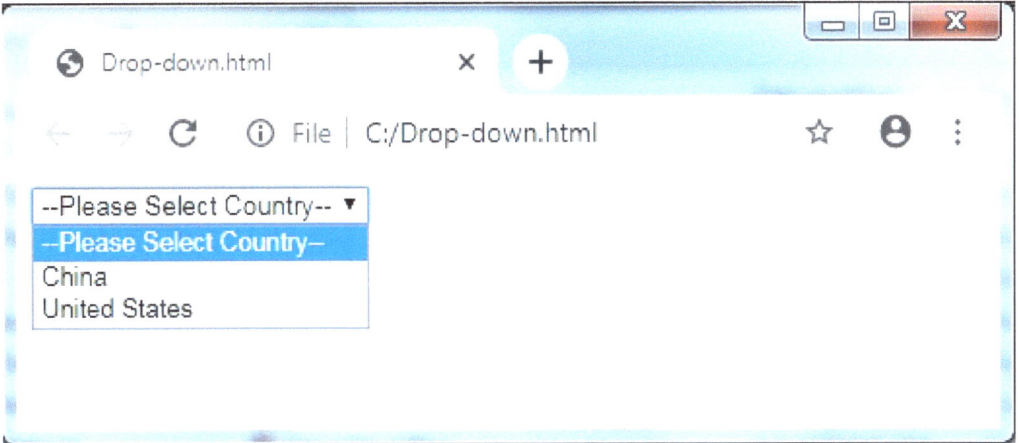

```html
<select id="country">
   <option value="">--Please Select Country--</option>
</select>

<script type="text/javascript">

   var countryArray=["China", "United States"];

   window.onload=function()
   {
      var countryObj=document.getElementById("country");

      for(var i=0;i<countryArray.length;i++)
      {
         var option=document.createElement("option");
         option.text=countryArray[i];
         option.value=countryArray[i];
         countryObj.options[countryObj.options.length]=option;
      }
   }

</script>
```

3. Add province options

selectedIndex: sets or returns the index of the selected option in a drop-down list.

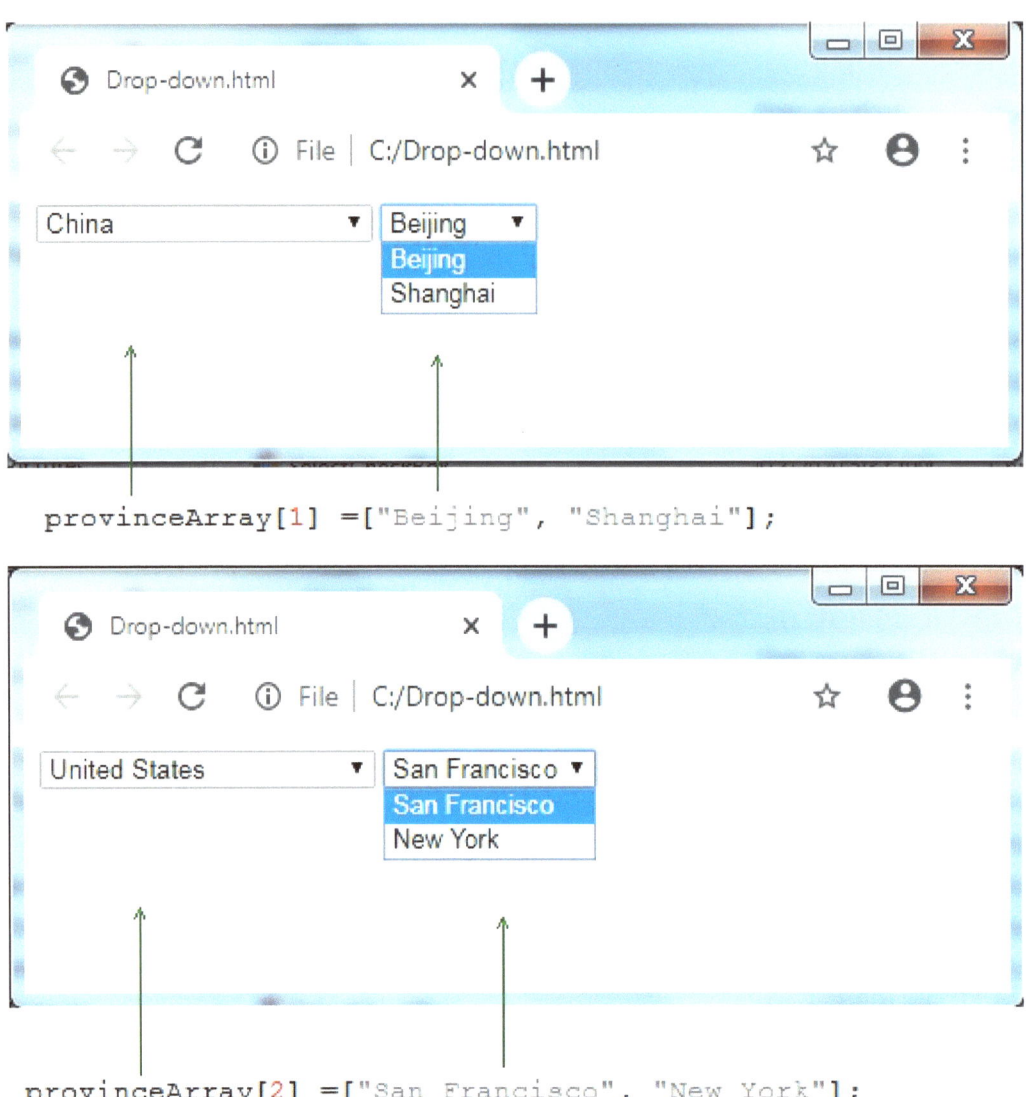

```html
<select id="country" onchange="doCountryChange(this)" >
  <option value="">--Please Select Country--</option>
</select>

<select id="province" >
</select>

<script type="text/javascript">
  var countryArray=["China", "United States"];

  var provinceArray = new Array();
  provinceArray[0] =[];
  provinceArray[1] =["Beijing", "Shanghai"];
  provinceArray[2] =["San Francisco", "New York"];

  window.onload=function()
  {
    var country=document.getElementById("country");
    for(var i=0;i<countryArray.length;i++)
    {
      var option=document.createElement("option");
      option.text=countryArray[i];
      option.value=countryArray[i];
      country.options[country.options.length]=option;
    }
  }

  function doCountryChange(obj)
  {
    var provinceObj=document.getElementById("province");
    provinceObj.options.length=0; // clear all
    var index=obj.selectedIndex;
    for(var i=0;i<provinceArray[index].length;i++)
    {
      var option=document.createElement("option");
      option.text=provinceArray[index][i];
      option.value=provinceArray[index][i];
      provinceObj.options[provinceObj.options.length]=option;
    }
  }
</script>
```

Event

Event List:

Onblur	element loses focus
Onchange	changes the contents
Onclick	mouse click on an object
Ondblclick	mouse double click on an object
Onerror	An error occurred while loading a document or image
Onfocus	element gets focus
Onkeydown	The key of a keyboard is pressed
Onkeypress	The key of a keyboard is pressed
Onkeyup	The key of a keyboard is released
Onload	a page or image is loaded
Onmousedown	a mouse button is pressed
Onmousemove	mouse is moved
Onmouseout	mouse is moved out from an element
Onmouseover	mouse is moved over an element
Onmouseup	mouse button is released
Onreset	reset button is clicked
Onresize	window or frame is resized
Onselect	text is selected
Onsubmit	submit button is clicked
Onunload	exit page

Login Web Page

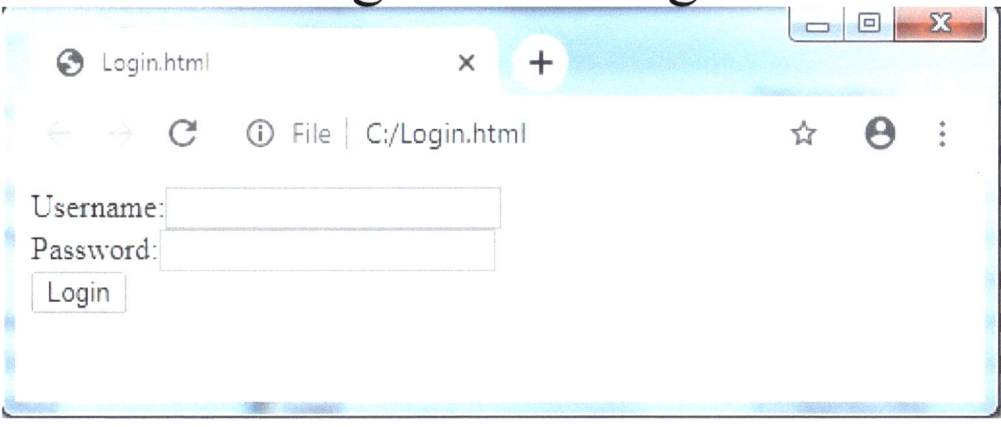

1. Create a Login.html file with Notepad and open it in your browser

```
Username:<input type="text" id="username" value="" /> <br>
Password:<input type="password" id="pwd" value="" /> <br>
<input type="button" value="Login" onclick="checkLogin()" />

<script type="text/javascript">
  function checkLogin()
  {
    var usernameObj=document.getElementById("username");
    var pwdObj=document.getElementById("pwd");

    if(usernameObj.value=="")
    {
      alert("Please input username !");
      return;
    }

    if(pwdObj.value=="")
    {
      alert("Please input password !");
      return;
    }

    alert("login successfull !");
  }
</script>
```

2. Create a Login.html file with Notepad and open it in your browser

document.onkeypress: the event occurs when the user presses a key.

```html
Username:<input type="text" id="username" value="" />
<br>
Password:<input type="password" id="pwd" value="" />
<br>
<input type="button" value="Login" onclick="checkLogin()" />

<script type="text/javascript">
   document.onkeypress=function(event)
   {
      var ext=window.event?window.event:event;
      var key=ext.keyCode?ext.keyCode:ext.which;
      if(key==13) // press enter key will be invoked
      {
         checkLogin();
      }
   }

   function checkLogin()
   {
      var usernameObj=document.getElementById("username");
      var pwdObj=document.getElementById("pwd");

      if(usernameObj.value=="")
      {
         alert("Please input username !");
         return;
      }

      if(pwdObj.value=="")
      {
         alert("Please input password !");
         return;
      }

      alert("login successfull !");
   }
</script>
```

MouseOver Thumbnail to Larger

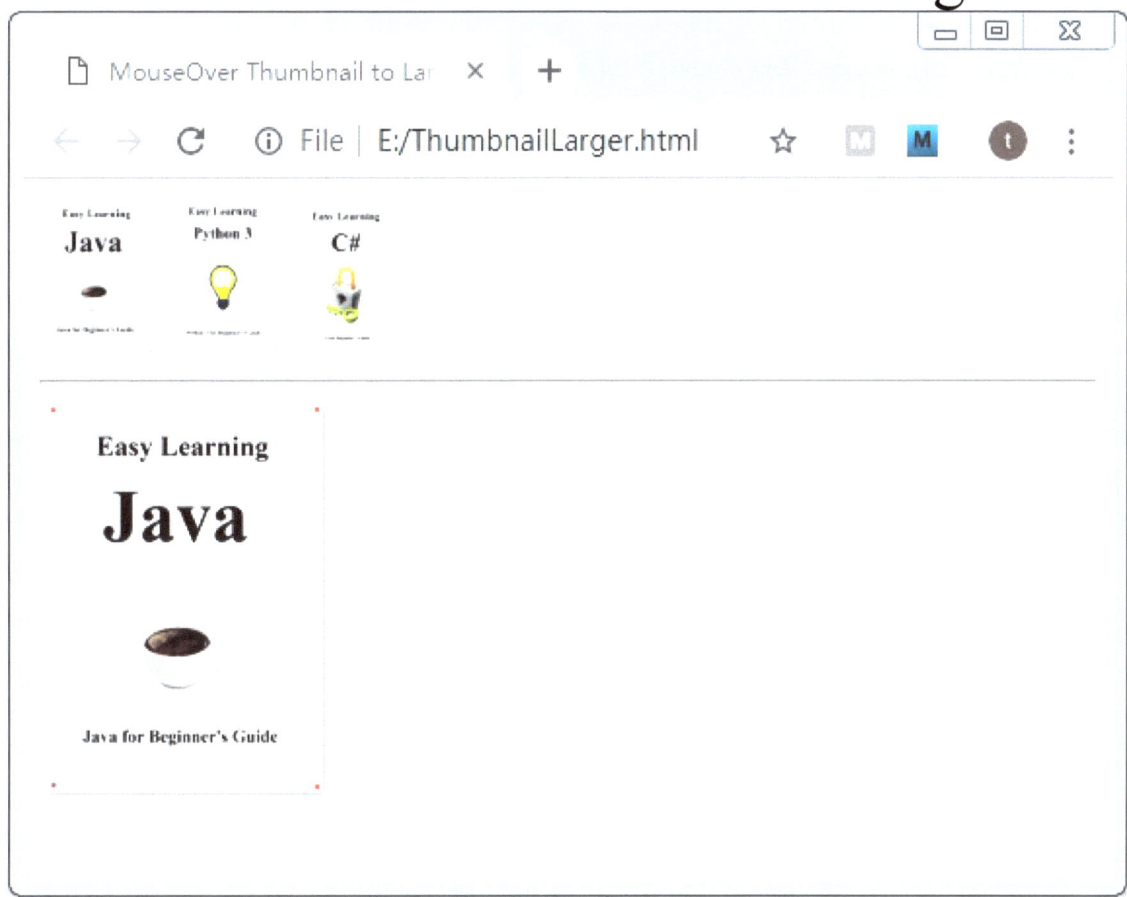

1. Create a ThumbnailLarger.html file with Notepad and open it in your browser

<img>: tag defines an image in an HTML page.

```html
<img src="images/java.jpg" width="60" onmouseover="zoomImage(this)" />
<img src="images/python.jpg" width="60" onmouseover="zoomImage(this)" />
<img src="images/csharp.jpg" width="60" onmouseover="zoomImage(this)" />
<hr>
<img id="image" src="" />
<script type="text/javascript">
  function zoomImage(obj)
  {
     document.getElementById("image").src = obj.src;
  }
</script>
```

CSS Inside Tag Style

CSS is a language that describes the style of an HTML document.

1. Create a InsideTagStyle.html

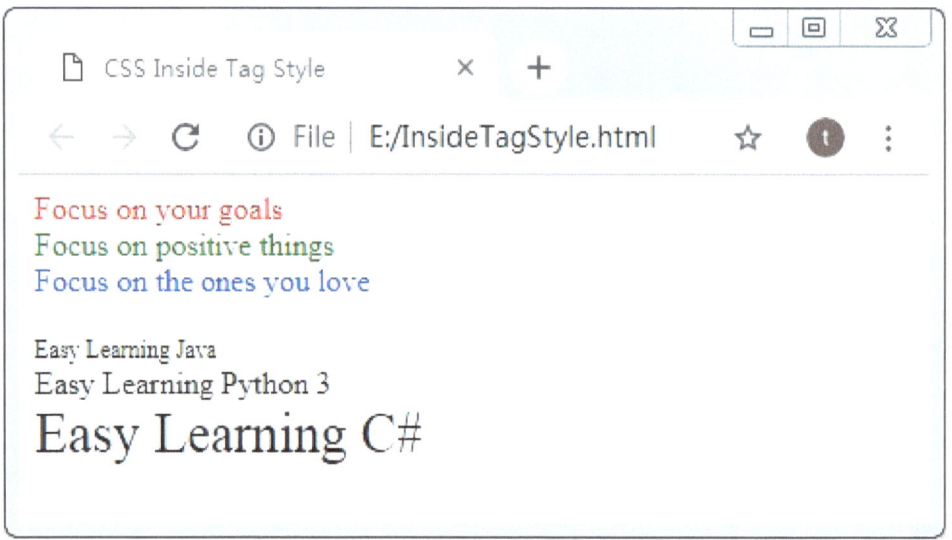

```
<div style="color:red">Focus on your goals</div>
<div style="color:green">Focus on positive things</div>
<div style="color:blue">Focus on the ones you love</div>

<br>

<div style="font-size:12px">Easy Learning Java</div>
<div style="font-size:16px">Easy Learning Python 3</div>
<div style="font-size:28px">Easy Learning C#</div>
```

CSS Inline Style

1. Create a InsideStyle.html

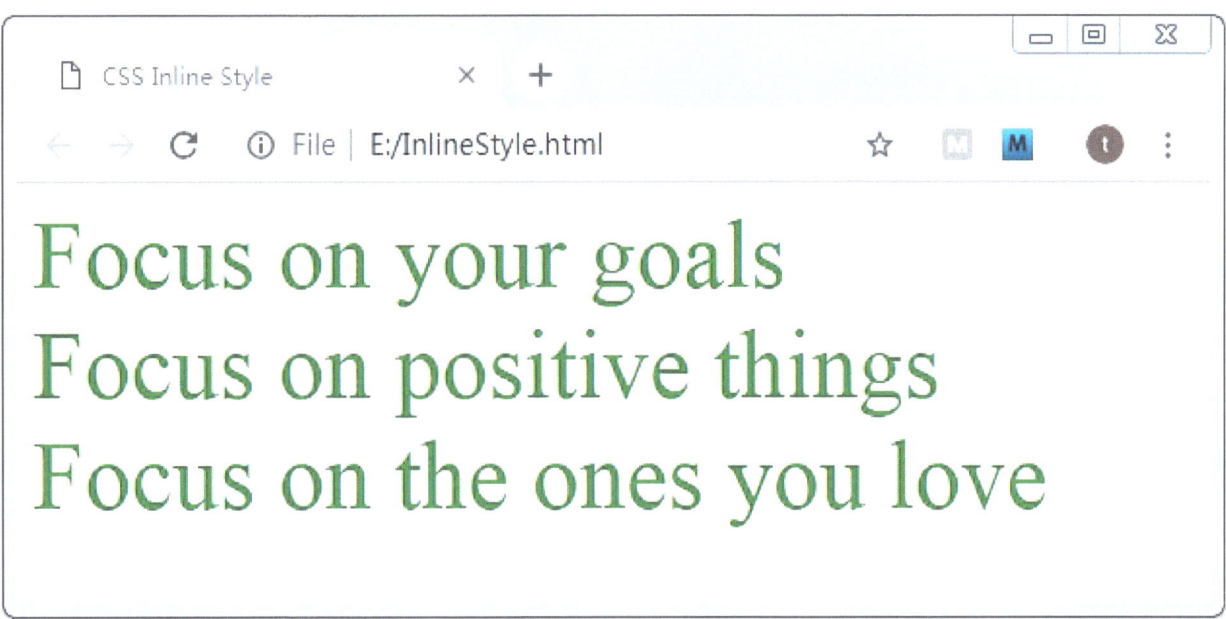

The .class selector: selects elements with a specific class attribute.

```
<style>
  .fontStyle{
     color:green;
     font-size:48px;
  }
</style>

<div class="fontStyle">Focus on your goals</div>
<div class="fontStyle">Focus on positive things</div>
<div class="fontStyle">Focus on the ones you love</div>
```

CSS Import Style

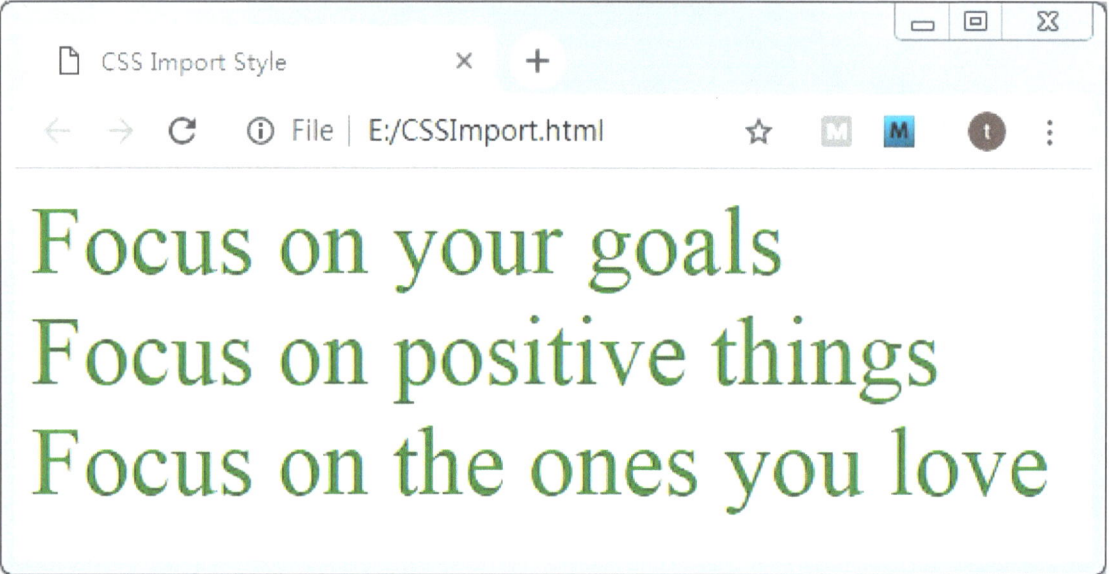

1. Create a style.css file

```
@CHARSET "UTF-8";

div{
  color:green;
  font-size:48px;
}
```

2. Create a CSSImport.html

<link>: tag defines a link between a document and an external resource style.css.

```
<link rel="stylesheet"  type="text/css" href="style.css" />

<div >Focus on your goals</div>
<div >Focus on positive things</div>
<div >Focus on the ones you love</div>
```

Class Reference Style

1. Create a CSSclass.html

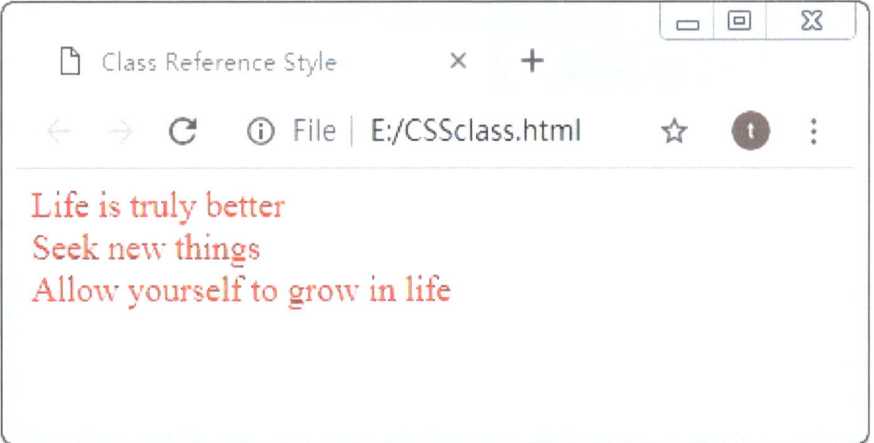

```
<style>
  .classStyleName{
    color:red;
    font-size:18px;
  }
</style>

<span class="classStyleName" >Life is truly better</span>
<br>

<span class="classStyleName" >Seek new things</span>
<br>

<span class="classStyleName" >Allow yourself to grow in life</span>
```

ID Reference Style

1. Create a CSSId.html

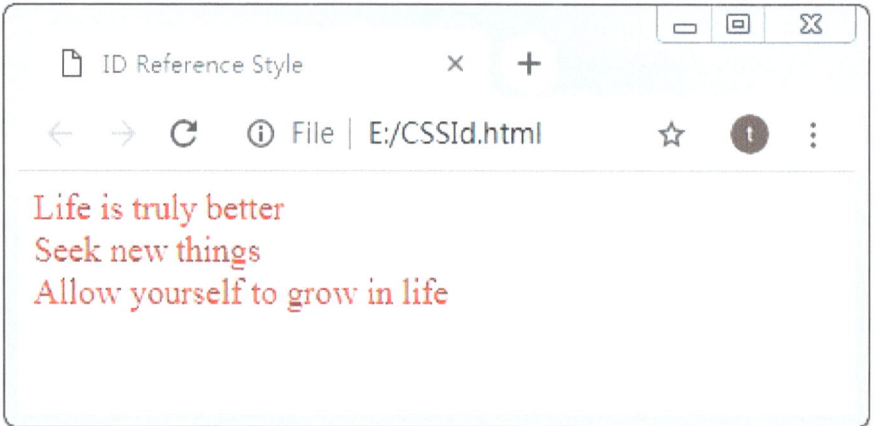

The #id selector: styles the element with the specified id.

```
<style>
  #IdStyleName{
     color:red;
     font-size:18px;
  }
</style>

<span id="IdStyleName" >Life is truly better</span>
<br>

<span id="IdStyleName" >Seek new things</span>
<br>

<span id="IdStyleName" >Allow yourself to grow in life</span>
```

CSS Font Style

1. Create a CSSFont.html

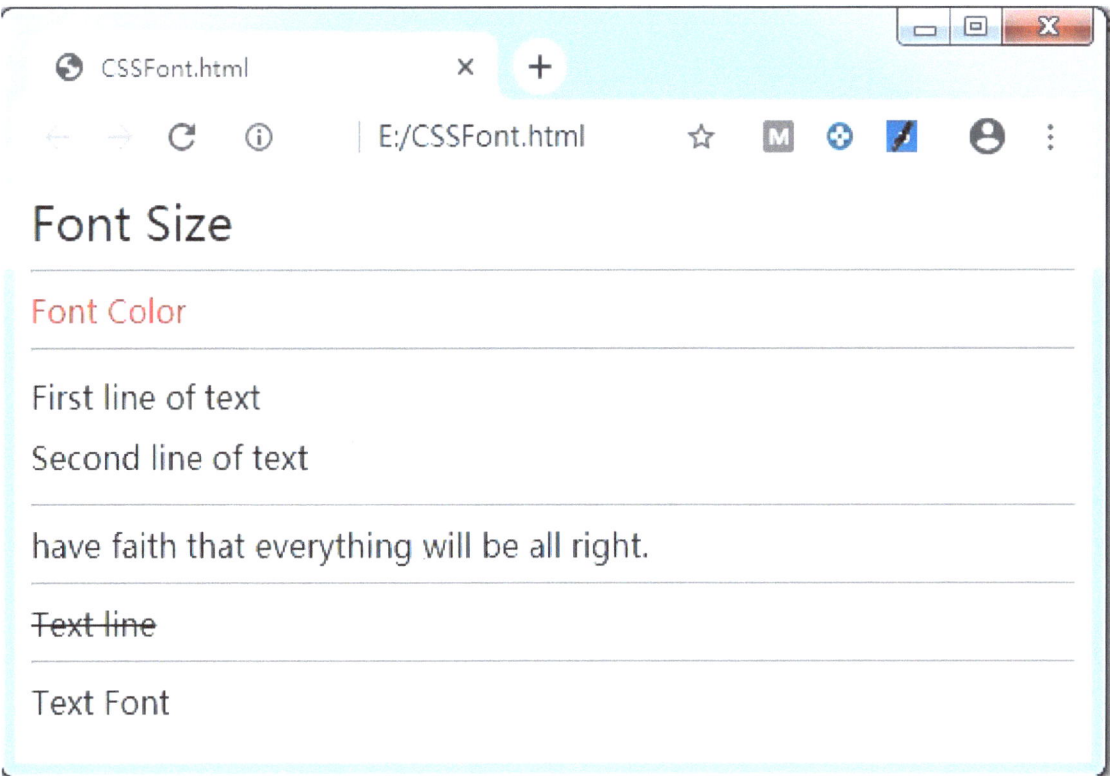

font-size:	specifies the size of the text inside
line-height:	specifies the height of a line
font-weight:	1.bold 2.normal
text-transform:	1.capitalize 2.uppercase 3.lowercase
text-decoration:	1.underline 2.overline 3.none
font-family:	"Times New Roman"

```html
<style>
  #fontSize{
    font-size:24px;
  }
  #fontColor{
    color:#ff0000;
  }
  #lineHeight{
    line-height: 30px;
  }
  #textTransform{
    text-transform: none;
  }
  #textDecoration{
    text-decoration: line-through;
  }
  #fontFamily{
    font-family: sans-serif;
  }
</style>

<span id="fontSize">Font Size</span>
<hr>

<span id="fontColor">Font Color</span>
<hr>

<span id="lineHeight">
    First line of text
    <br>
    Second line of text
</span>
<hr>

<span id="textTransform">have faith that everything will be all right.</span>
<hr>

<span id="textDecoration">Text line</span>
<hr>

<span id="fontFamily">Text Font</span>
```

CSS Background Style

1. Create a BackgroundAttribute.html

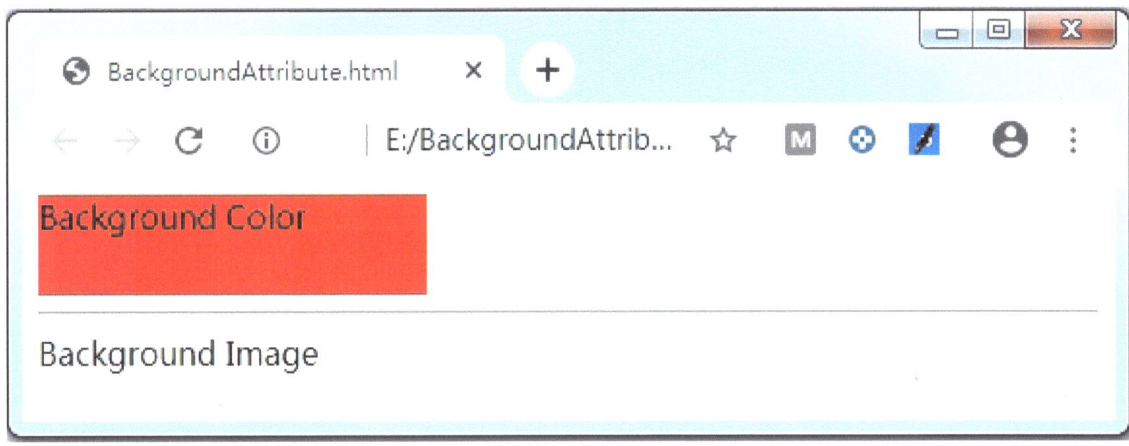

background-color: #FFFFFF;   background color
background-image: url();   picture url
background-repeat: no-repeat;   1.no-repeat 2.no-repeat-x 3.no-repeat-y
background-position: 1.left 2.top

```
<style>
  #backgroundColor{
    background-color: #ff0000;
    width:200px;
    height:50px;
  }

  #backgroundImage{
    background-image: url("images/cat.gif");
    background-repeat: no-repeat;
    background-position: right;
  }
</style>

<div id="backgroundColor">Background Color</div>
<hr>
<div id="backgroundImage">Background Image</div>
```

CSS Border Style

1. Create a BorderAttribute.html

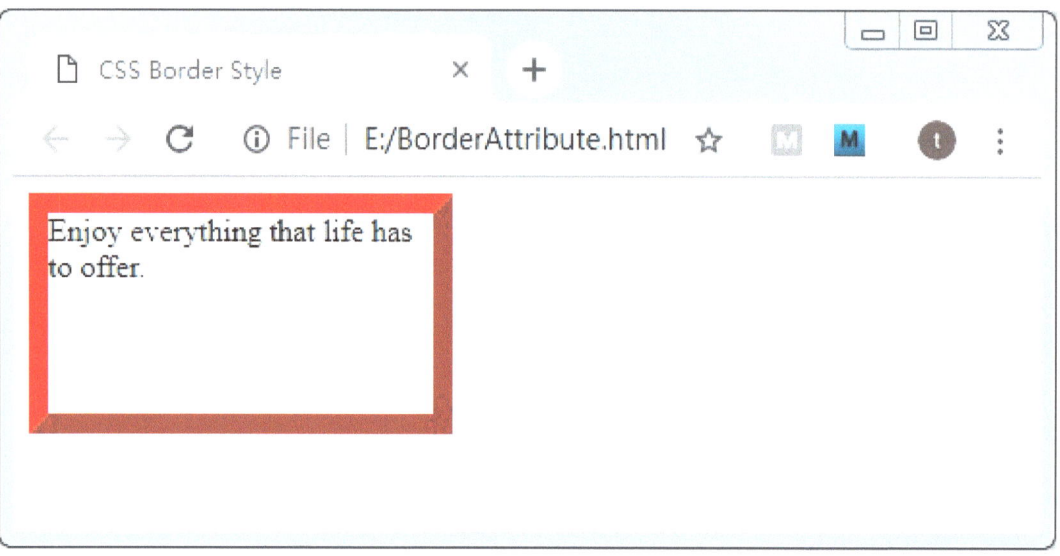

border-style: 1.dotted 2.dashed 3.solid 4.double
5.groove 6.ridge 7.inset 8.outset

```html
<style>
  #borderStyle{
    width:200px;
    height:100px;
    border-color:#ff0000;
    border-width:10px;
    border-style:outset;
  }
</style>

<div id="borderStyle">Enjoy everything that life has to offer.</div>
```

CSS Spacing Style

1. Create a SpacingStyle.html

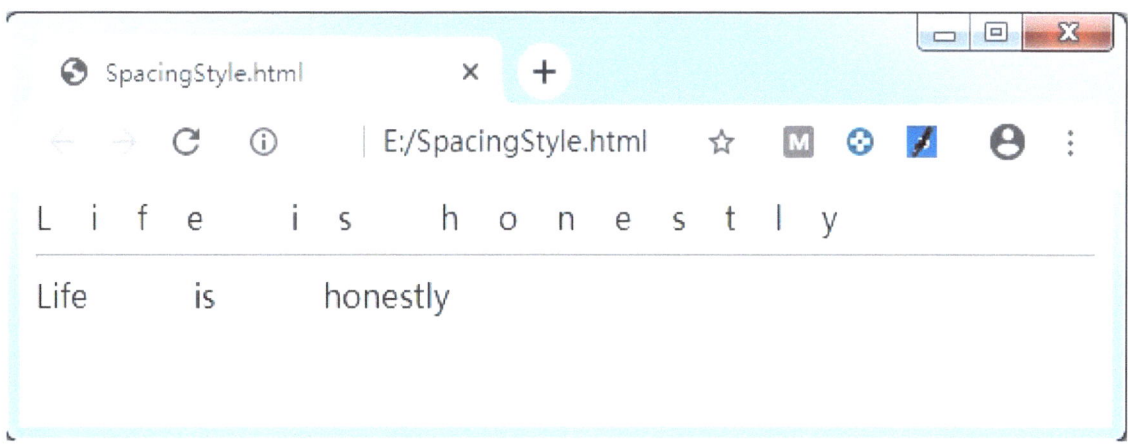

letter-spacing: increases or decreases the space between characters in a text.
word-spacing: increases or decreases the white space between words.

```
<style>
  #letterSpacing{
     letter-spacing: 20px;
  }

  #wordSpacing{
     word-spacing: 50px;
  }
</style>

<div id="letterSpacing">Life is honestly</div>
<hr>

<div id="wordSpacing">Life is honestly</div>
```

2. Create a SpacingStyle2.html

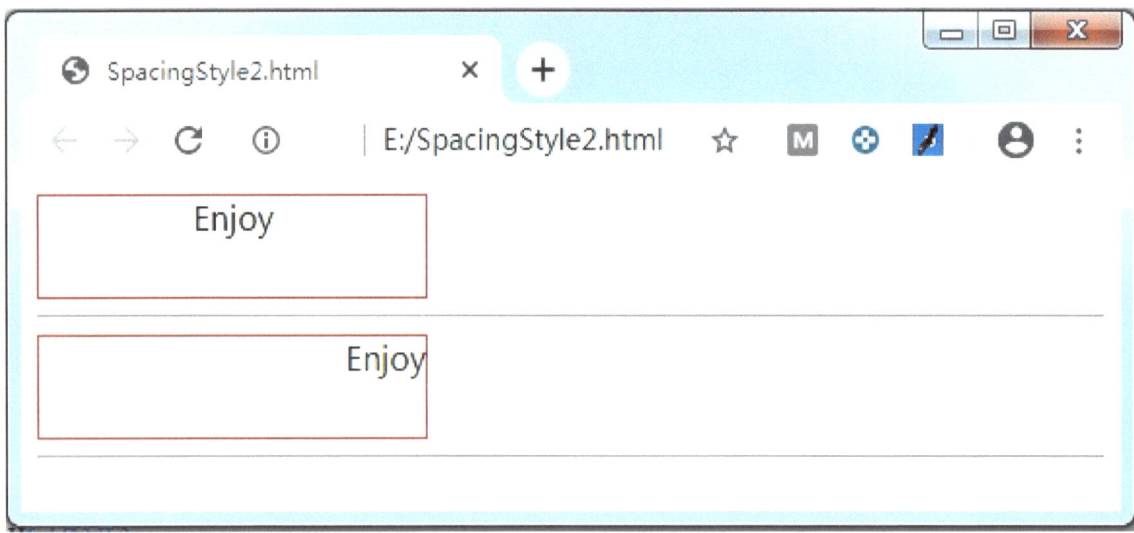

text-align: 1.justify 2.left 3.right 4.center

```
<style>
  #textAlignCenter{
    text-align:center;
    width:200px;
    height:50px;
    border: 1px solid #ff0000;
  }

  #textAlignRight{
    text-align:right;
    width:200px;
    height:50px;
    border: 1px solid #ff0000;
  }
</style>

<div id="textAlignCenter">Enjoy</div>
<hr>

<div id="textAlignRight">Enjoy</div>
<hr>
```

CSS Inner and Outer Margins

1. Create a Margins.html

margin: Outer Margins
1 margin-top
2 margin-bottom
3 margin-left
4 margin-right

```
<style>
  #marginDiv{
    width:200px;
    height:50px;
    border:1px solid #ff0000;
    margin-top:20px;
  }
</style>

<div id="marginDiv">
  Friends is always there.
</div>

<div id="marginDiv">
  Friends is always there.
</div>
```

2. Create a Margins2.html

padding: Inner Margins
padding-top
padding-bottom
padding-left
padding-right

```
<style>
  #paddingDiv{
    width:200px;
    height:100px;
    border:1px solid #ff0000;
    padding-top:30px;
  }
</style>

<div id="paddingDiv">
  Friends is always there.
</div>
```

CSS List Style

1. Create a ListStyle.html

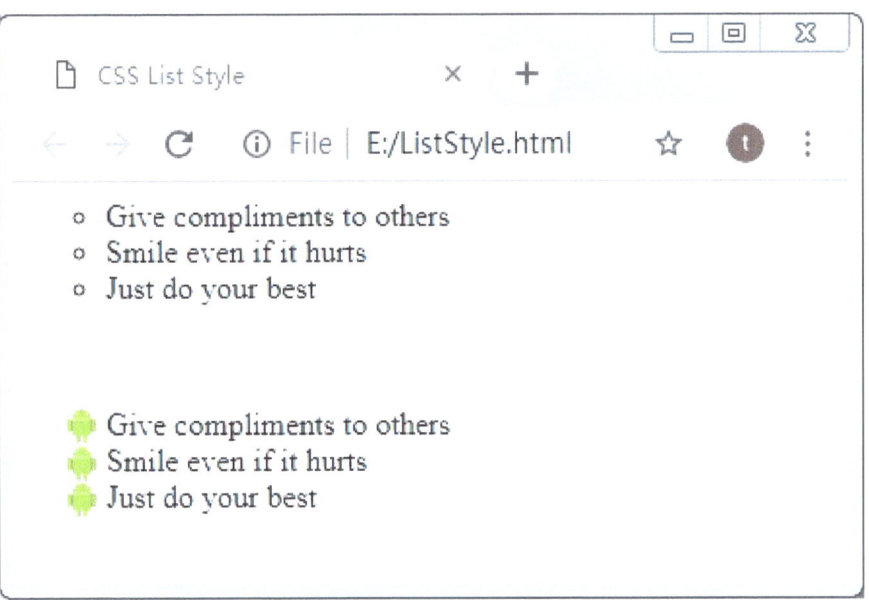

list-style-type: 1.disc 2.circle 3.square 4.decimal 5.lower-roman
                         6.upper-roman 7.lower-alpha 8.upper-alpha
list-style-position: 1.outside 2.inside
list-style-image: url(..); picture

```
<style>
  #list{
    list-style-type: circle;
    list-style-position:outside;
  }

  #listImage{
    list-style-type: circle;
    list-style-position:outside;
    list-style-image: url(images/icon.jpg);
  }
</style>
```

```html
<ul id="list">
   <li>Give compliments to others</li>
   <li>Smile even if it hurts</li>
   <li>Just do your best</li>
</ul>

<br>

<ul id="listImage">
   <li>Give compliments to others</li>
   <li>Smile even if it hurts</li>
   <li>Just do your best</li>
</ul>
```

CSS Float

1. Create a CSSFloat.html

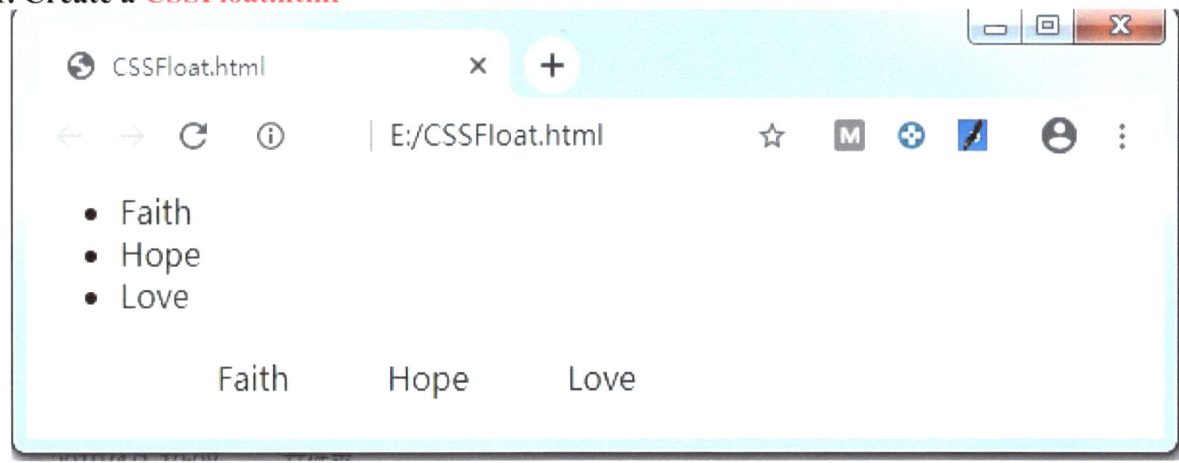

float: specifies how an element should float.

```
<style>
   #floatStyle li{
      float:left;
      padding-left:50px;
      list-style:none;
   }
</style>

<ul>
   <li>Faith</li>
   <li>Hope</li>
   <li>Love</li>
</ul>

<br>

<ul id="floatStyle">
   <li>Faith</li>
   <li>Hope</li>
   <li>Love</li>
</ul>
```

CSS Position Style

1. Create a PositionStyle.html

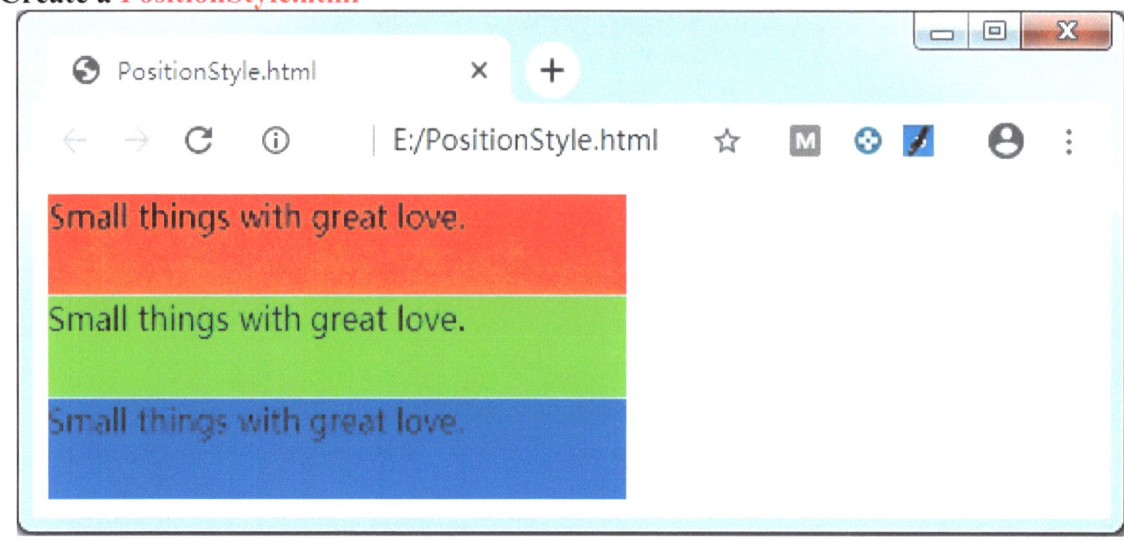

```
<style>
  #redBox{
    width:300px;
    height:50px;
    background-color:#ff0000;
    margin-top:1px;
  }
  #greenBox{
    width:300px;
    height:50px;
    background-color:#00ff00;
    margin-top:1px;
  }
  #blueBox{
    width:300px;
    height:50px;
    background-color:#0000ff;
    margin-top:1px;
  }
</style>
<div id="redBox">Small things with great love.</div>
<div id="greenBox">Small things with great love.</div>
<div id="blueBox">Small things with great love.</div>
```

2. Change greenBox position: absolute

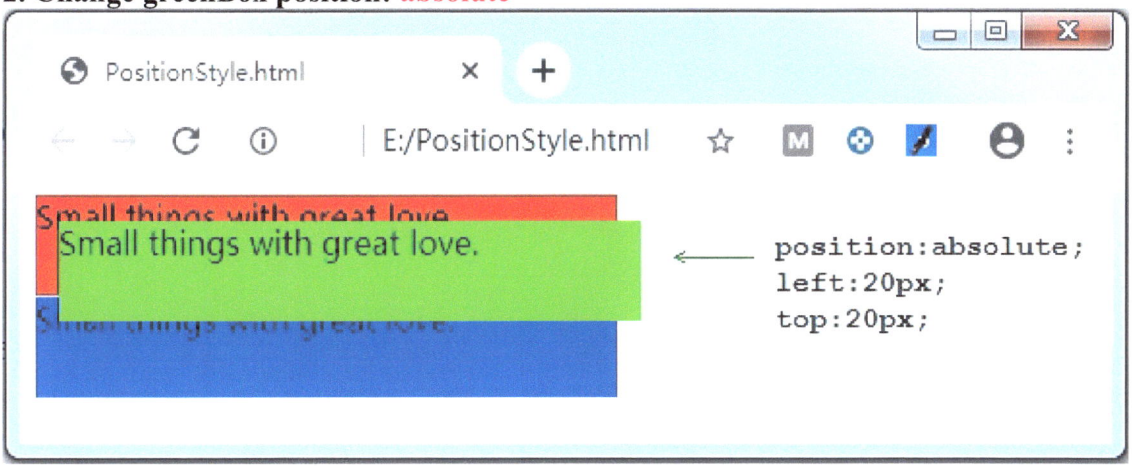

```
<style>
  #redBox{
    width:300px;
    height:50px;
    background-color:#ff0000;
    margin-top:1px;
  }
  #greenBox{
    width:300px;
    height:50px;
    background-color:#00ff00;
    margin-top:1px;
    position:absolute;
    left:20px;
    top:20px;
  }
  #blueBox{
    width:300px;
    height:50px;
    background-color:#0000ff;
    margin-top:1px;
  }
</style>
<div id="redBox">Small things with great love.</div>
<div id="greenBox">Small things with great love.</div>
<div id="blueBox">Small things with great love.</div>
```

3. Change greenBox position: relative

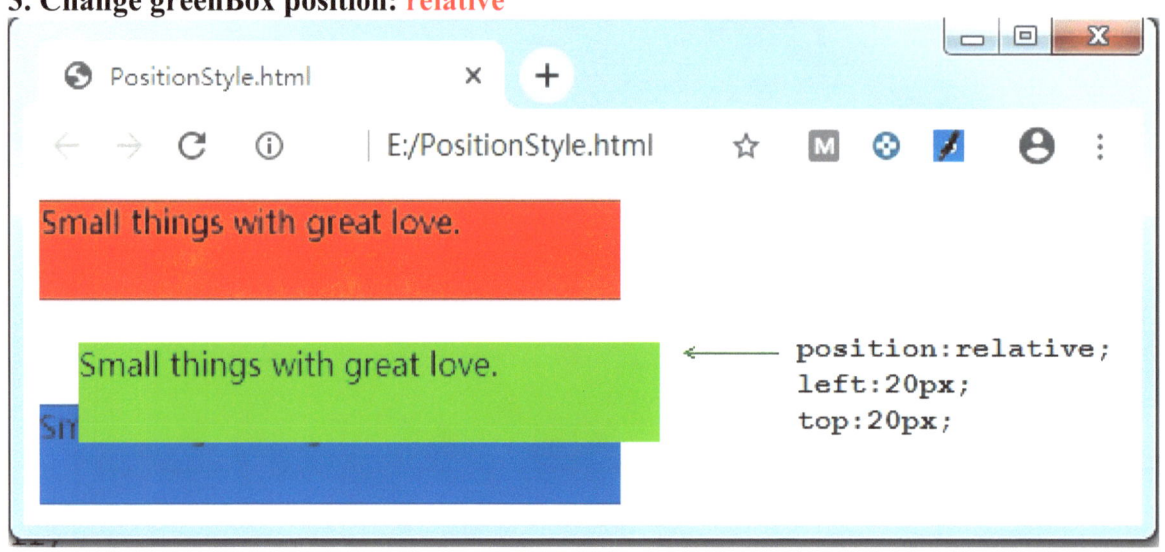

```
<style>
  #redBox{
    width:300px;
    height:50px;
    background-color:#ff0000;
    margin-top:1px;
  }
  #greenBox{
    width:300px;
    height:50px;
    background-color:#00ff00;
    margin-top:1px;
    position:relative;
    left:20px;
    top:20px;
  }
  #blueBox{
    width:300px;
    height:50px;
    background-color:#0000ff;
    margin-top:1px;
  }
</style>
<div id="redBox">Small things with great love.</div>
<div id="greenBox">Small things with great love.</div>
<div id="blueBox">Small things with great love.</div>
```

CSS Visibility Style

1. Create a **VisibilityStyle.html**

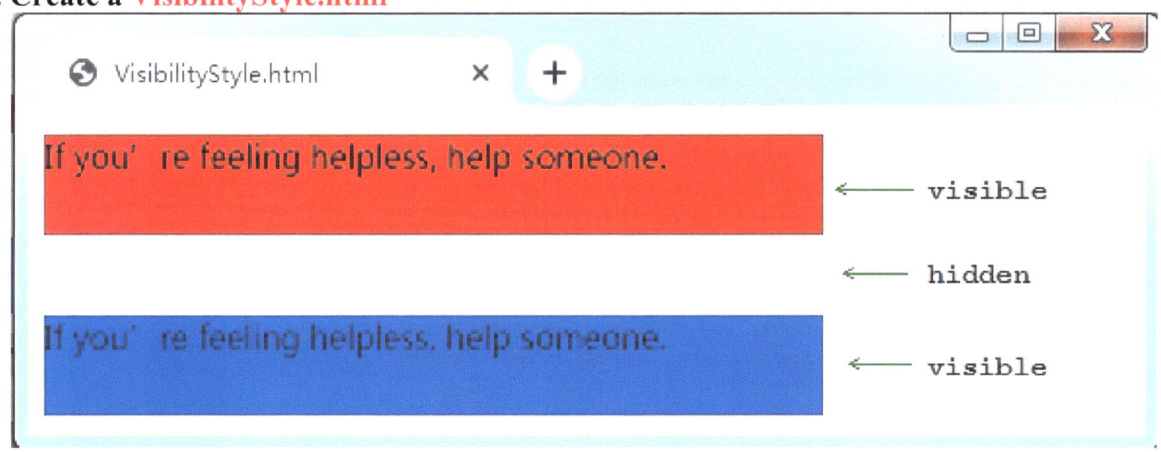

```
<style>
  #redBox{
    width:400px;
    height:50px;
    background-color:#ff0000;
    margin-top:1px;
    visibility: visible
  }
  #greenBox{
    width:400px;
    height:50px;
    background-color:#00ff00;
    margin-top:1px;
    visibility: hidden
  }
  #blueBox{
    width:400px;
    height:50px;
    background-color:#0000ff;
    margin-top:1px;
    visibility: visible
  }
</style>
<div id="redBox">If you're feeling helpless, help someone.</div>
<div id="greenBox">If you're feeling helpless, help someone.</div>
<div id="blueBox">If you're feeling helpless, help someone.</div>
```

2. Create a ScrollStyle.html

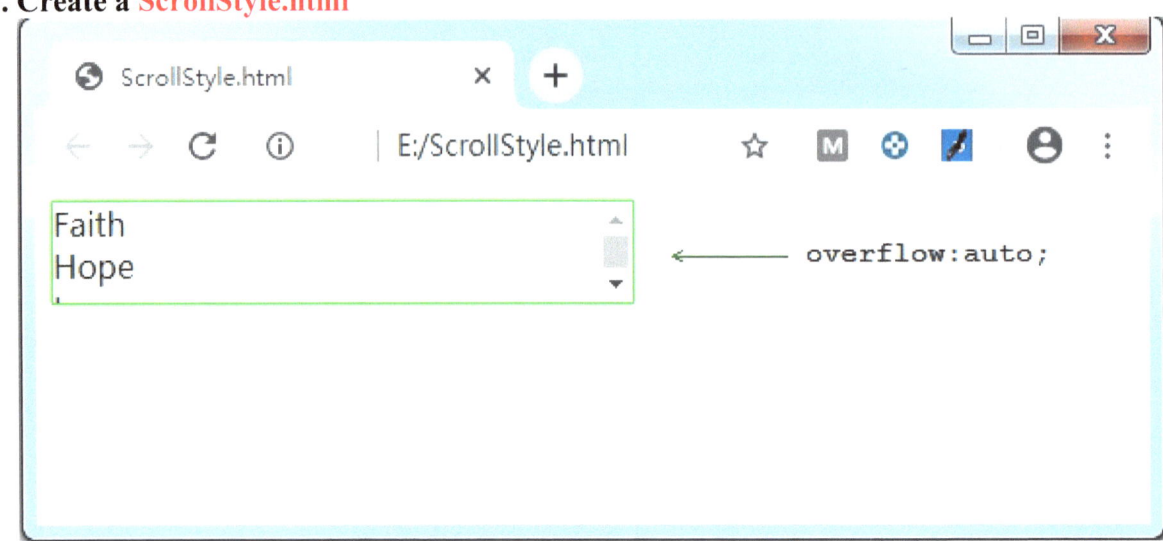

```
<style>
  #greenBox{
    width:300px;
    height:50px;
    border:1px solid #00ff00;
    margin-top:1px;
    overflow:auto;
  }
</style>

<div id="greenBox">
  Faith <br>
  Hope <br>
  Love <br>
  Joy <br>
  Peace
</div>
```

CSS Association Style

1. Create a CSSAssociation.html

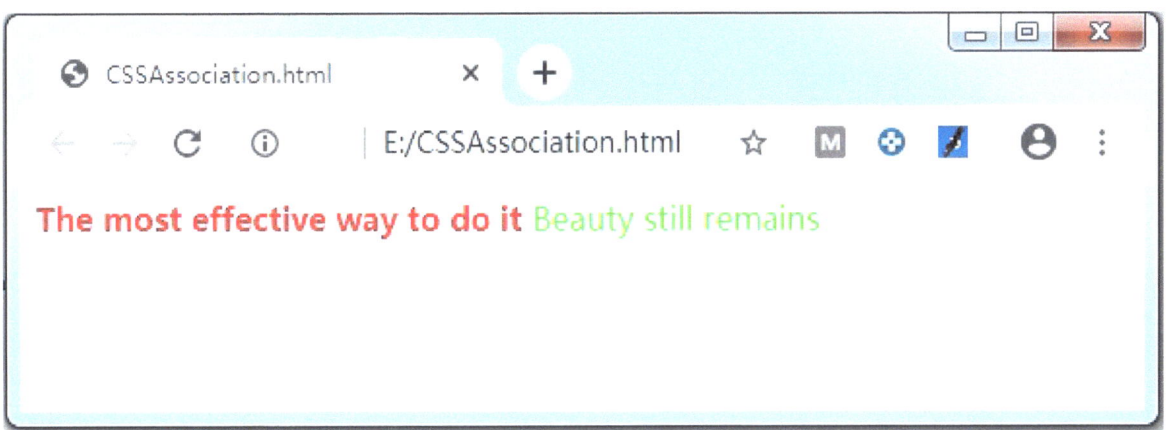

```
<style>
 div{
   color:#ff0000;
 }

 div span{
   color:#00ff00;
 }
</style>

<div>
   <b>The most effective way to do it</b>
   <span> Beauty still remains</span>
</div>
```

2. Create a CSSAssociation.html

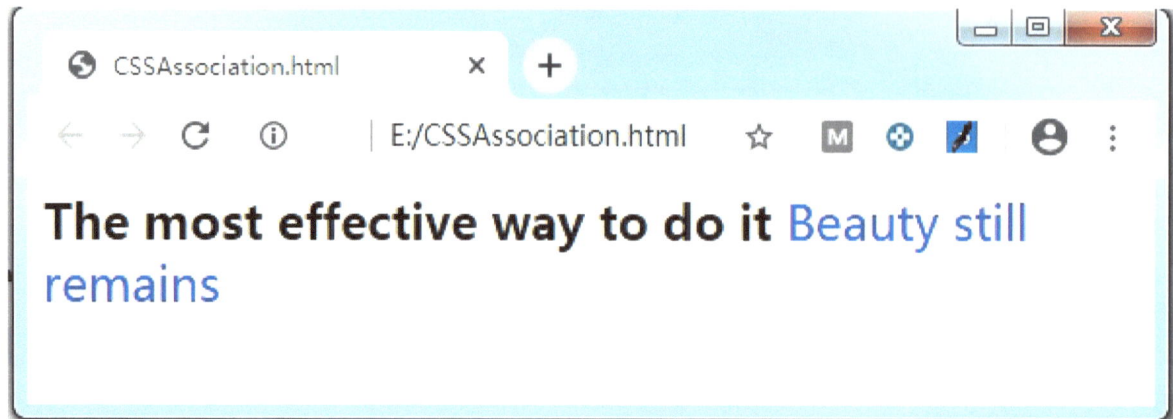

```
<style>
   .div1{
      font-size:24px;
   }

   .div1 span{
      color:#0000ff;
   }
</style>

<div class="div1">
   <b>The most effective way to do it</b>
   <span> Beauty still remains</span>
</div>
```

3. Create a CSSAssociation.html

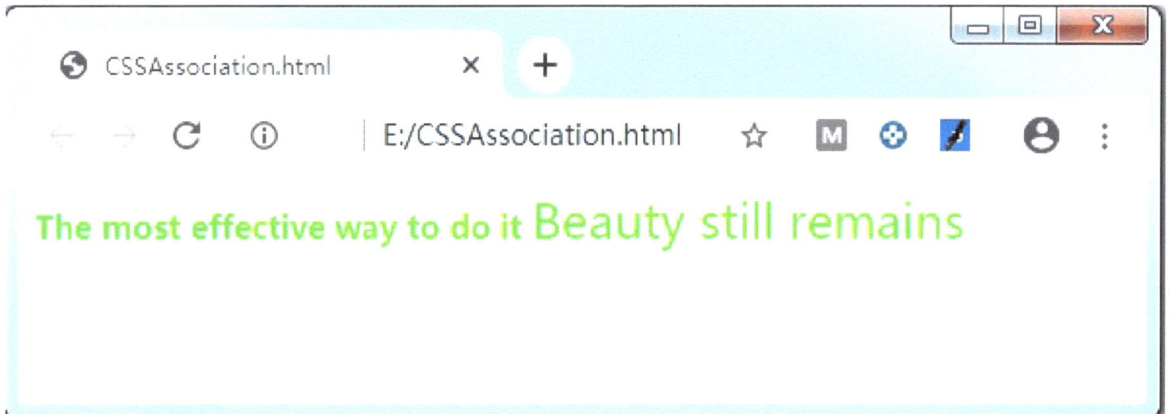

```
<style>
   #div2{
      color:#00ff00;
   }

   #div2 span{
      font-size:24px;
   }
</style>

<div id="div2">
   <b>The most effective way to do it</b>
   <span> Beauty still remains</span>
</div>
```

CSS Hyperlink Style

1. **Create a HyperlinkStyle.html**

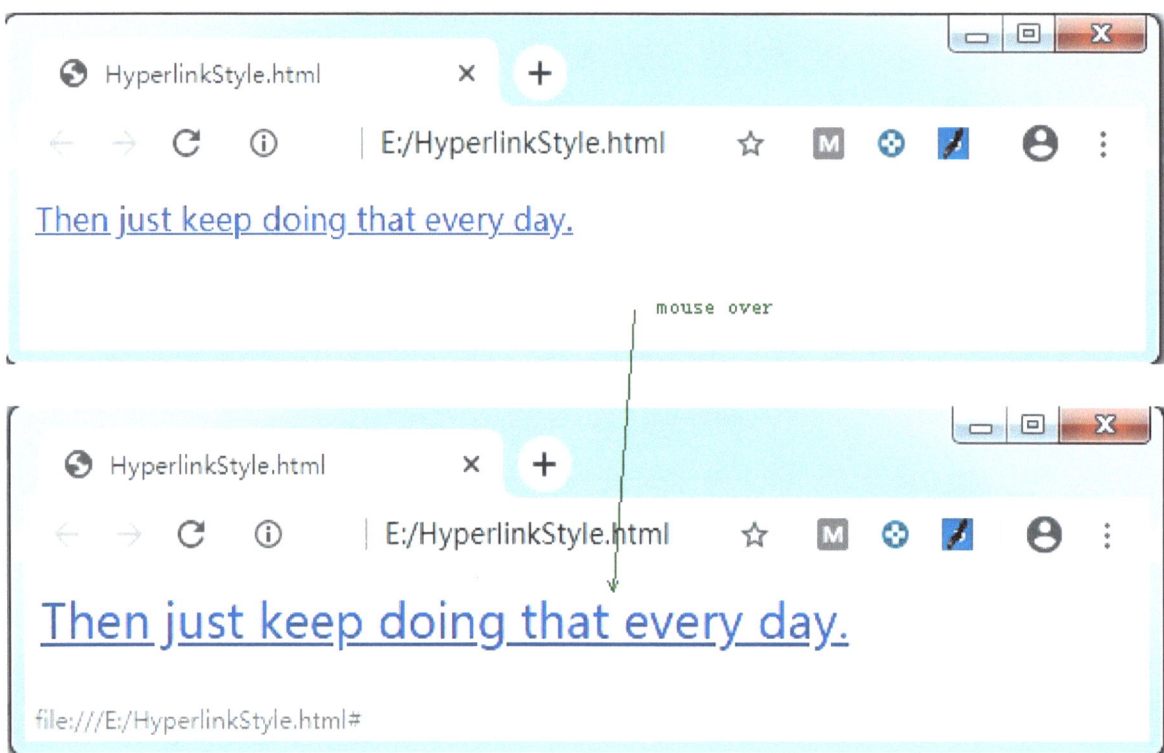

a:link   when hyperlink no clicked
a:visited after the hyperlink is clicked
a:hover   when the cursor moves to the hyperlink
a:active   when hyperlink is clicked

```
<style>
 a:link{ }
 a:visited{ color:#0000ff; }
 a:hover{font-size:24px;}
 a:active{color:#00ff00;}

 input.focus{background-color: #0000ff;}
</style>

<a href="#">Then just keep doing that every day.</a>
```

CSS Union Style

1. Create a CSSUnion.html

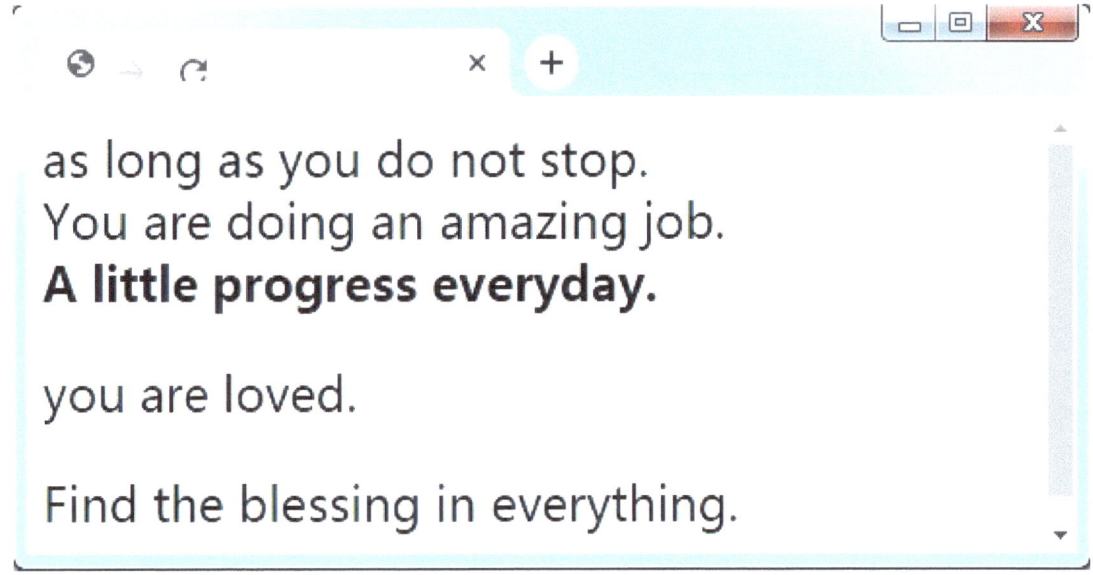

```
<style>
  span,div,.className,#idName{
    font-size:24px;
  }
</style>

<span>as long as you do not stop.</span>

<div>You are doing an amazing job.</div>

<b class="className">A little progress everyday.</b>

<p id="idName">you are loved.</p>

<div><p>Find the blessing in everything.</p></div>
```

Element Hierarchy

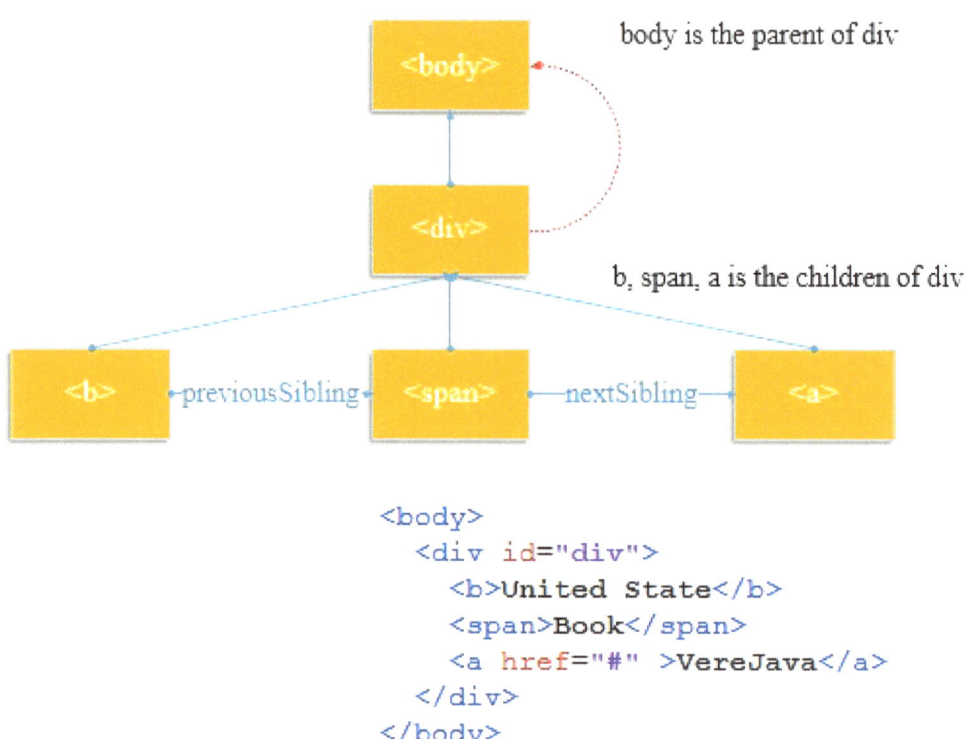

```
<body>
  <div id="div">
    <b>United State</b>
    <span>Book</span>
    <a href="#" >VereJava</a>
  </div>
</body>
```

1. Change ElementHierarchy.html to get all child nodes.

obj.childNodes: get all child nodes of current node
obj. nodeName: get the node's name
obj. nodeType: get the node's type
obj. innerHTML: get the node's html content

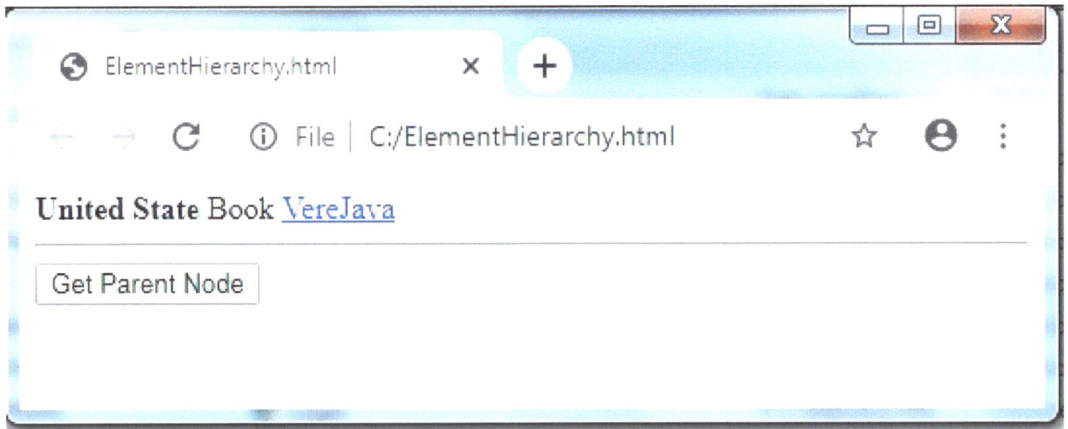

<b>: tag specifies bold text.
<a>: tag defines a hyperlink, which is used to link from one page to another.

```html
<body>
  <div id="div">
    <b>United State</b>
    <span>Book</span>
    <a href="#" >VereJava</a>
  </div>
  <hr>
  <input type="button" value="Get Parent Node" onclick="doGetParentNode()" />
</body>

<script type="text/javascript">
  function doGetParentNode()
  {
     var divObj=document.getElementById("div");
     alert(divObj.parentNode.nodeName);
  }
</script>
```

2. Change ElementHierarchy.html get all child nodes

obj.childNodes: get all child nodes of current node
obj.nodeName: get the parent node's name
obj.nodeType: get the parent node's type
obj.innerHTML: get the parent node's html content

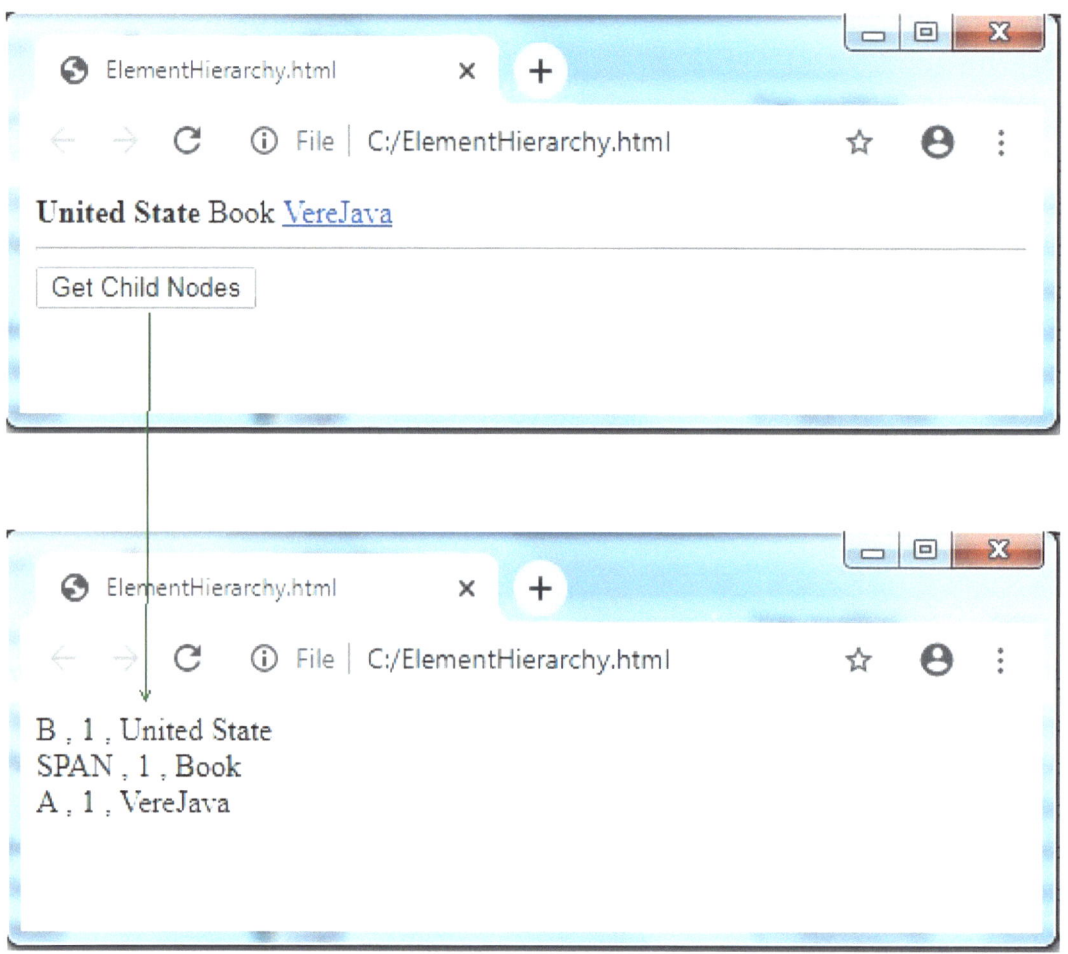

```html
<body>
  <div id="div">
   <b>United State</b>
   <span>Book</span>
   <a href="#" >VereJava</a>
  </div>
  <hr>
  <input type="button" value="Get Child Nodes" onclick="doGetChildNodes()" />
</body>

<script type="text/javascript">

  function doGetChildNodes()
  {
     var div=document.getElementById("div");
     var childNodes=div.childNodes;
     for(var i=0;i<childNodes.length;i++)
     {
        if(childNodes[i].nodeType==1)
        {
           document.write(childNodes[i].nodeName+" , ");
           document.write(childNodes[i].nodeType+" , ");
           document.write(childNodes[i].innerHTML+"<br>");
        }
     }
  }
</script>
```

3. Change ElementHierarchy.html get book node's previous and next node

obj. previousSibling: get previous node of current node
obj. nextSibling: get next node of current node

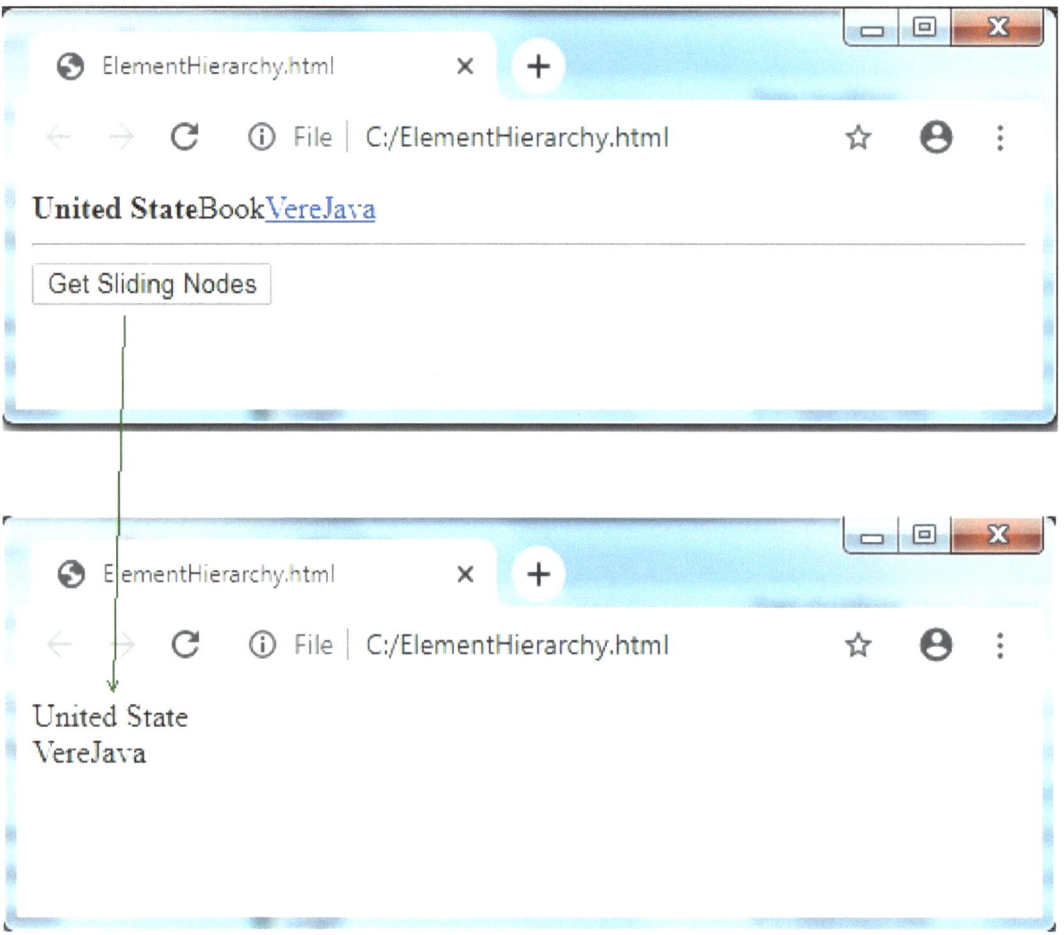

```html
<body>
 <div id="div">
   <b>United State</b><span id="book">Book</span><a href="#" >VereJava</a>
 </div>
 <hr>
 <input type="button" value="Get Sliding Nodes" onclick="doGetSliding()" />
</body>

<script type="text/javascript">

   function doGetSliding()
   {
      var bookObj=document.getElementById("book");
      document.write(bookObj.previousSibling.innerHTML+"<br>");
      document.write(bookObj.nextSibling.innerHTML);
   }

</script>
```

Create Text Node

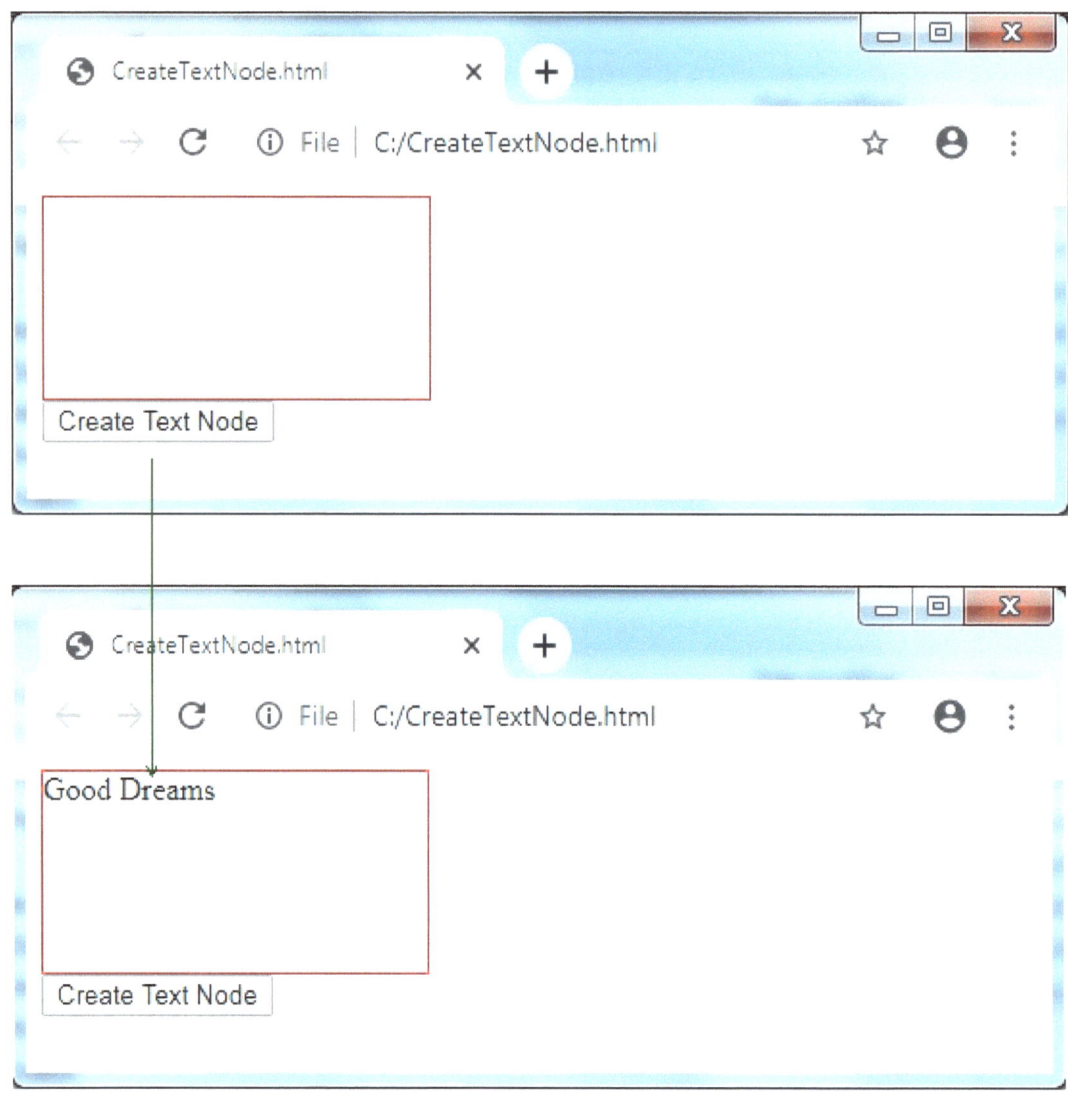

1. Create a CreateTextNode.html file with Notepad and open it in your browser

obj. createTextNode: creates a Text Node with the specified text
obj. appendChild: appends a node as the last child of a node

```html
<style>
   div{
      width:200px;
      height:100px;
      border:1px solid #ff0000;
   }
</style>

<div id="div"></div>
<input type="button" value="Create Text Node" onclick="doCreateTextNode()" />

<script type="text/javascript">

   function doCreateTextNode()
   {
      var divObj = document.getElementById("div");
      var newNode=document.createTextNode("Good Dreams");
      divObj.appendChild(newNode);
   }

</script>
```

2. Create a CreateElement.html file with Notepad and open it in your browser

obj. createElement: creates an Element Node with the specified name
obj. appendChild: appends a node as the last child of a node

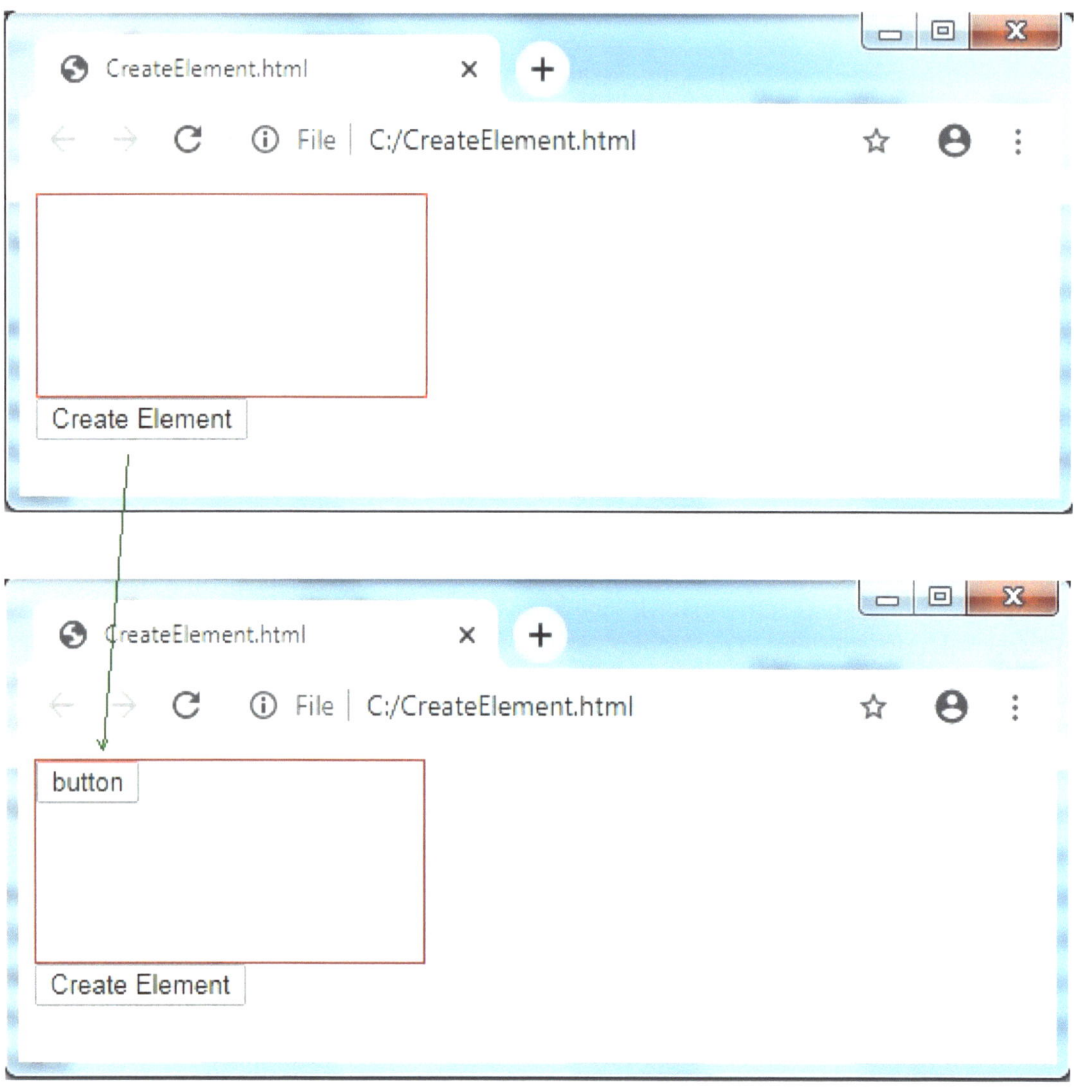

```html
<style>
    div{
        width:200px;
        height:100px;
        border:1px solid #ff0000;
    }
</style>

<div id="div">
</div>

<input type="button" value="Create Element" onclick="doCreateElement()" />

<script type="text/javascript">

    function doCreateElement()
    {
        var divObj = document.getElementById("div");
        var buttonElement=document.createElement("input");
        buttonElement.type="button";
        buttonElement.value="button";
        divObj.appendChild(buttonElement);
    }

</script>
```

Delete Node

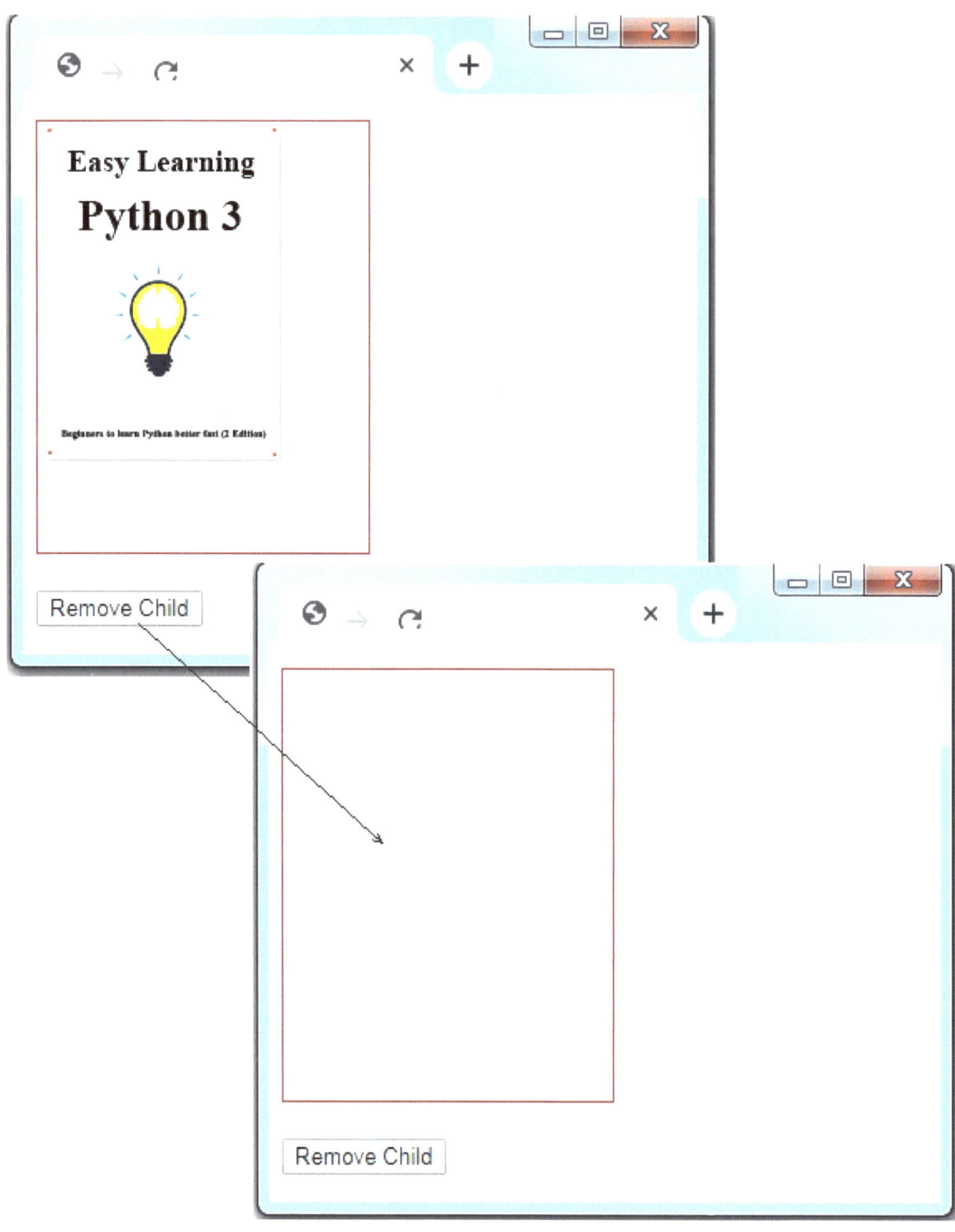

1. Create a DeleteNode.html file with Notepad and open it in your browser

obj. removeChild: removes a specified child node

```html
<style>
   div{
      width:200px;
      height:250px;
      border:1px solid #ff0000;
   }
</style>

<div id="div1">
   <img id="image" src="python.jpg" />
</div>
<br>
<input type="button" value="Remove Child" onclick="doRemoveChild()" />

<script type="text/javascript">

   function doRemoveChild()
   {
      var div=document.getElementById("div1");
      var img=document.getElementById("image");
      div.removeChild(img);
   }

</script>
```

Replace Node

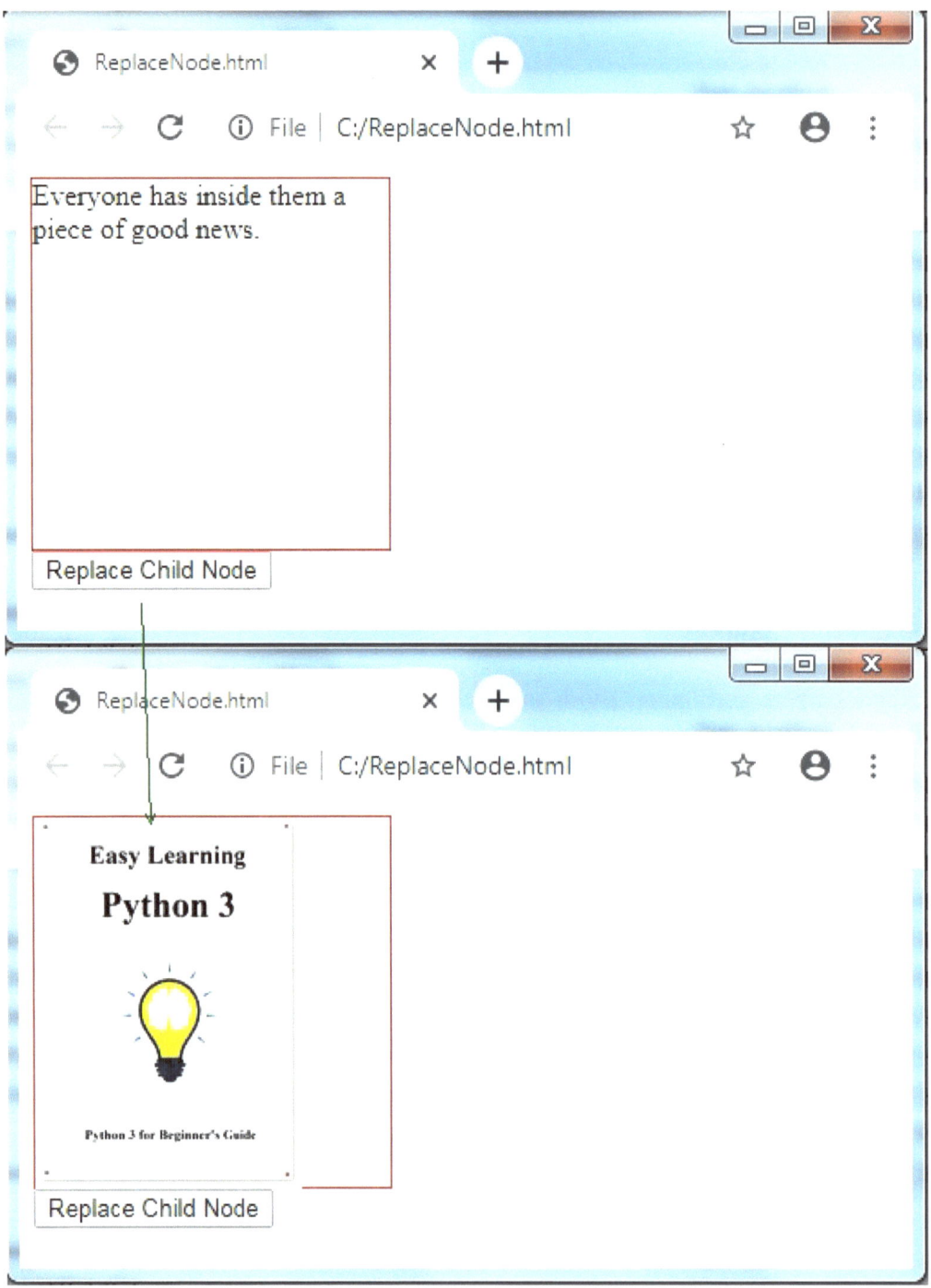

1. Create a ReplaceNode.html file with Notepad and open it in your browser

obj. replaceChild: replaces a child node with a new node

```html
<style>
   #div1{
      width:200px;
      height:200px;
      border:1px solid #ff0000;
   }
</style>

<div id="div1">Everyone has inside them a piece of good news.</div>
<input type="button" value="Replace Child Node" onclick="doReplaceChild()" />

<script type="text/javascript">

   function doReplaceChild()
   {
      var imgNode=document.createElement("img");
      imgNode.src="python.jpg";
      var div1=document.getElementById("div1");
      div1.replaceChild(imgNode,div1.childNodes[0]);
   }

</script>
```

Add Contact Example

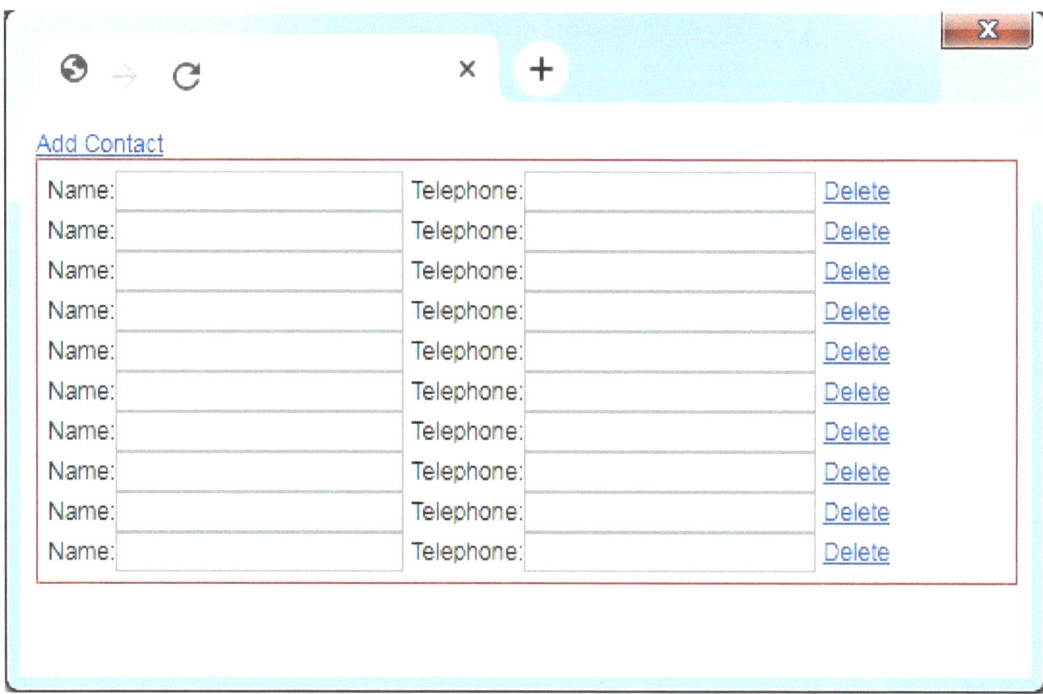

1. Create a AddContactExample.html file with Notepad and open it in your browser

```html
<style>
  #div{
    border:1px solid #ff0000;
    width:550px;
  }
</style>

<a href="javascript:void(0)" onclick="addContact()" >Add Contact</a>
<div id="div">
  <div id="contact">
    Name:<input type="text" name="user" />
    Telephone:<input type="text" name="telephone" />
    <a href="javascript:void(0)" onclick="deleteNode(this)" >Delete</a>
  </div>
</div>

<script type="text/javascript">

  function addContact()
  {
    var contact=document.getElementById("contact");
    var newNone=contact.cloneNode(true);

    var div=document.getElementById("div");
    div.appendChild(newNone);
  }

  function deleteNode(obj)
  {
    if(obj.parentNode.parentNode.childNodes.length>1)
      obj.parentNode.removeNode(true);
  }

</script>
```

CSS Style Font

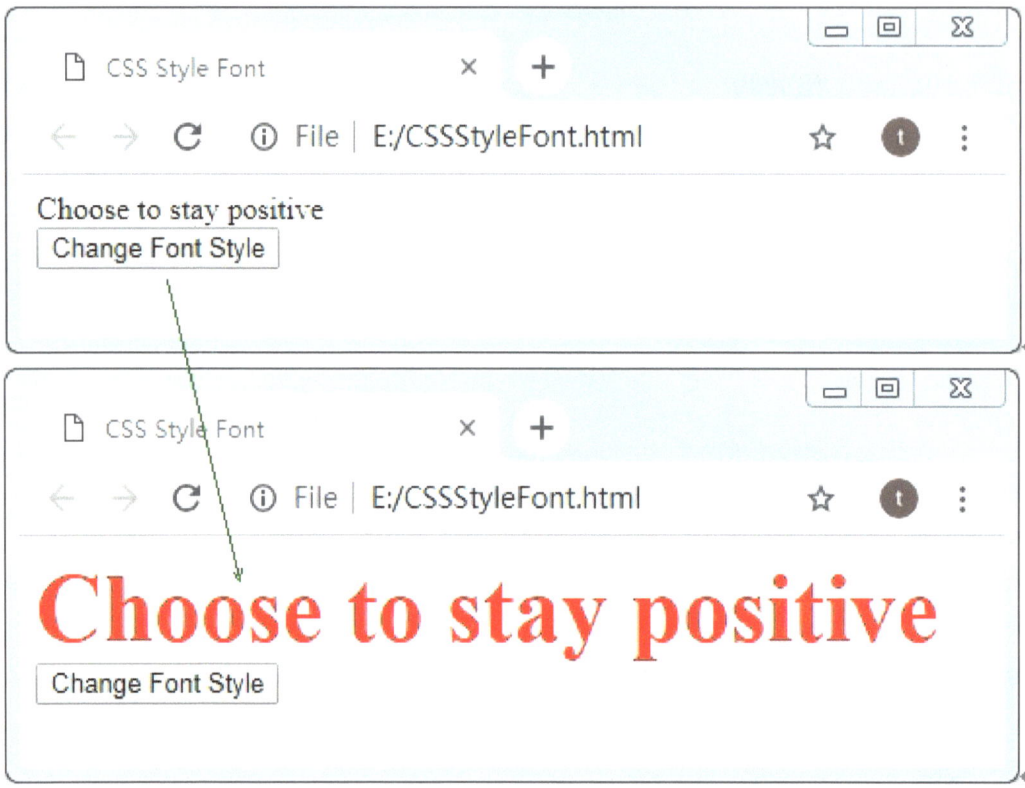

1. Create a CSSStyleFont.html file with Notepad and open it in your browser

```html
<div id="div">Choose to stay positive</div>
<input type="button" value="Change Font Style" onclick="doChangeFont()" />

<script type="text/javascript">
  function doChangeFont()
  {
     var div=document.getElementById("div");
     div.style.fontSize=48+"px";
     div.style.fontWeight="bold";
     div.style.color="#ff0000";
  }
</script>
```

CSS Change Class Selector

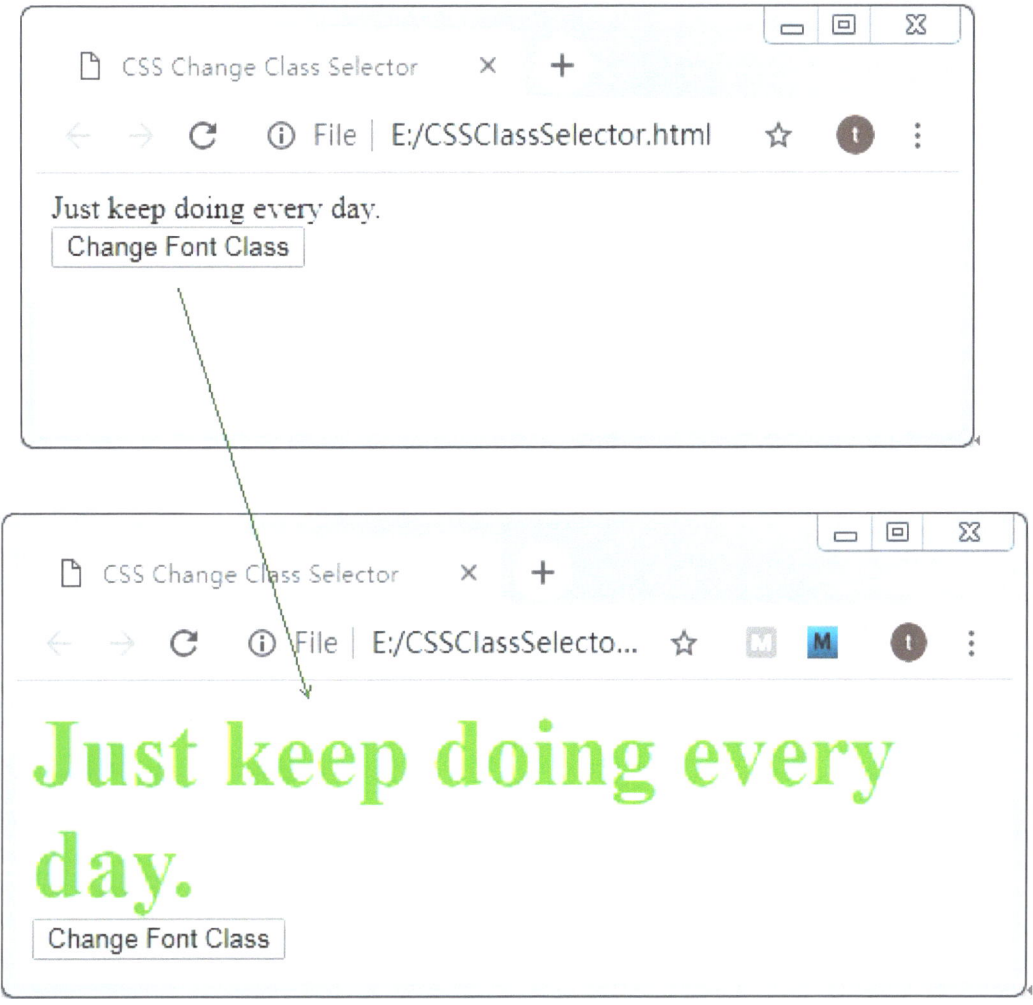

1. Create a CSSClassSelector.html file with Notepad and open it in your browser

```html
<style type="text/css">
  .smallFont{
    font-size:12px;
    color:#ff0000;
  }
  .bigFont{
    font-size:48px;
    font-weight:bold;
    color:#00ff00;
  }
</style>

<div id="div">Just keep doing every day.</div>
<input type="button" value="Change Font Class" onclick="changeFont()" />

<script type="text/javascript">

  function changeFont()
  {
    var div=document.getElementById("div");
    if(div.className=="smallFont")
    {
      div.className="bigFont";
    }
    else
    {
      div.className="smallFont";
    }
  }

</script>
```

CSS Overflow Expand and Close

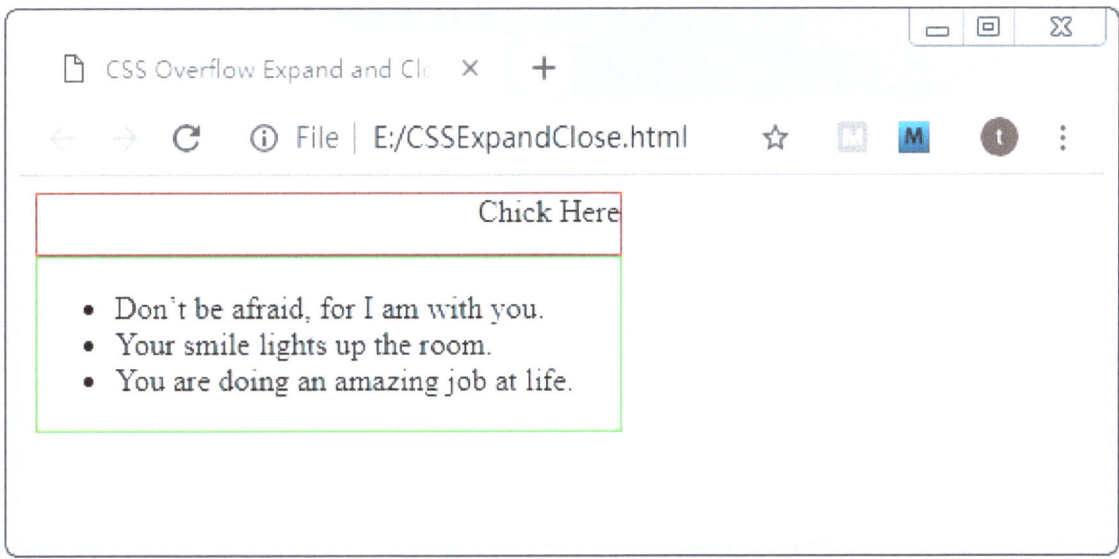

1. Create a CSSExpandClose.html file with Notepad and open it in your browser

```
<style type="text/css">
  .open{
    display :"" ;
  }

  .close{
    display :none ;
  }

  #div{
    width:300px;
    height:30px;
    border:1px solid #ff0000;
    text-align:right;
  }

  #div2{
    width:300px;
    border:1px solid #00ff00;
  }
</style>
```

```html
<div id="div" onclick="change()">Chick Here</div>
<div id="div2">
<ul>
 <li>Don't be afraid, for I am with you. </li>
 <li>Your smile lights up the room.</li>
 <li>You are doing an amazing job at life.</li>
</ul>
</div>

<script type="text/javascript">

   function change()
   {
      var div2=document.getElementById("div2");
      if(div2.className=="open")
      {
         div2.className="close";
      }
      else
      {
         div2.className="open";
      }
   }

</script>
```

CSS Floating Highlighting

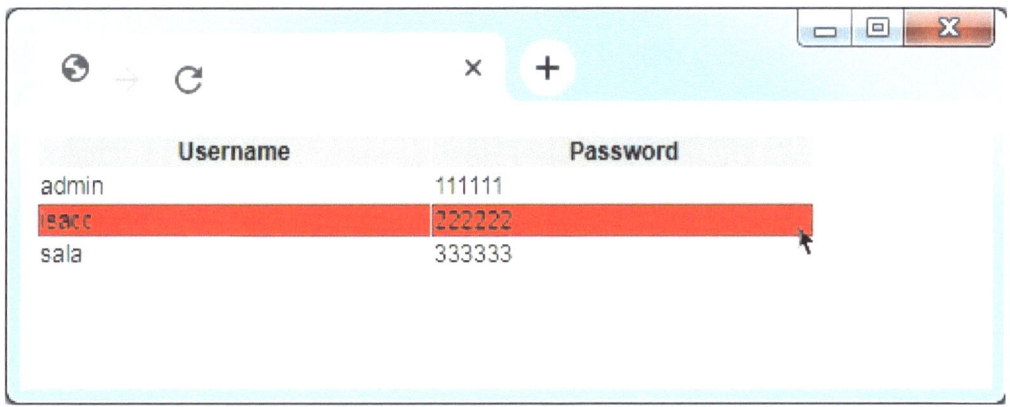

1. Create a CSSHighlighting.html file with Notepad and open it in your browser

```
<style type="text/css">
  .over{
    background-color: #ff0000;
  }

  .down{
    background-color: #0000ff;
  }

  table{
    border:1px solid #eeeeee;
    width:400px;
    border-collapse: collapse;
  }

  table th{
    border:1px solid #eeeeee;
    background-color: #cccccc;
  }

  table td{
    border:1px solid #eeeeee;
  }
</style>
```

```html
<table>
  <tr>
    <th>Username</th><th>Password</th>
  </tr>
  <tr onmousedown="doDown(this)" onmouseover="doOver(this)" onmouseout="doOut(this)">
    <td>admin</td><td>111111</td>
  </tr>
  <tr onmousedown="doDown(this)" onmouseover="doOver(this)" onmouseout="doOut(this)">
    <td>isacc</td><td>222222</td>
  </tr>
  <tr onmousedown="doDown(this)" onmouseover="doOver(this)" onmouseout="doOut(this)">
    <td>sala</td><td>333333</td>
  </tr>
</table>

<script type="text/javascript">

  function doOver(obj){
     if(obj.className!="down"){
        obj.className="over";
     }
  }

  function doOut(obj){
     if(obj.className!="down"){
        obj.className="";
     }
  }

  function doDown(obj){
     if(obj.className!="down"){
        obj.className="down";
     }else{
        obj.className="over";
     }
  }

</script>
```

Table Create Rows Columns

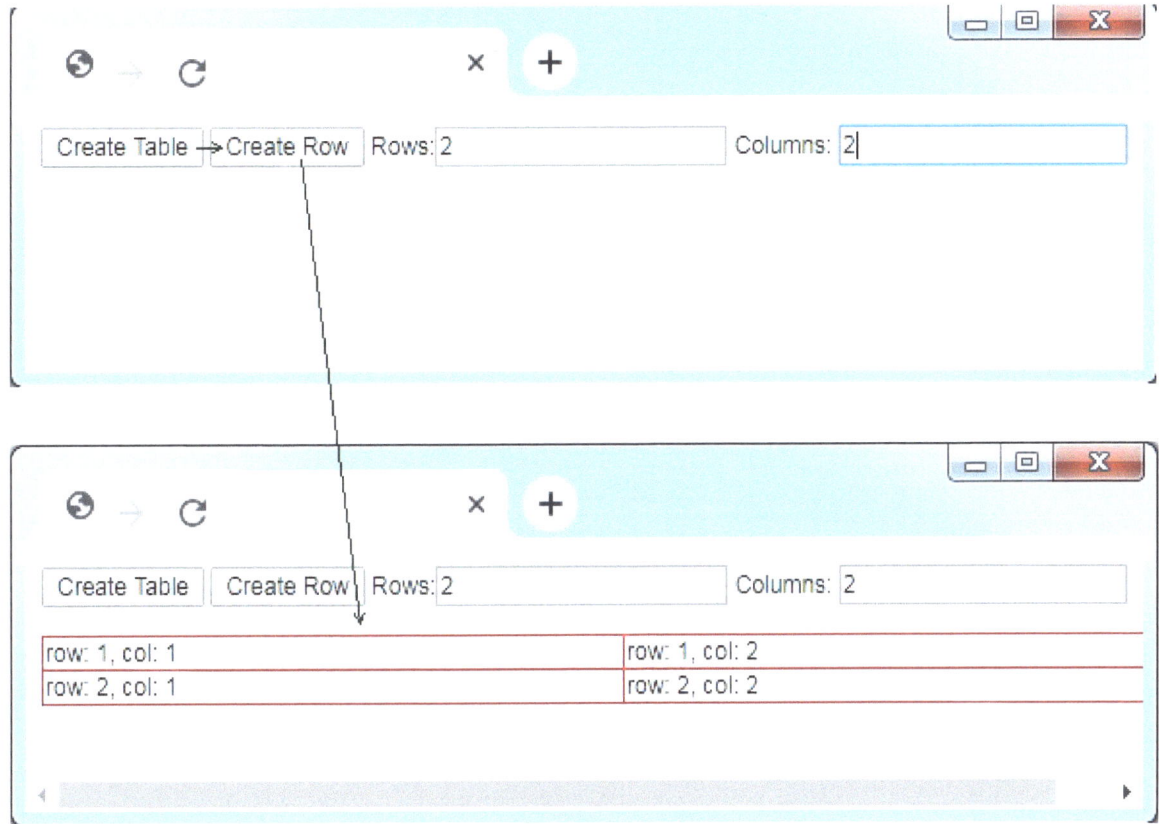

1. Create a **TableCreate RowsColumns.html** file with **Notepad** and open it in your browser

table.insertRow: inserts a new row (<tr>) in a given <table>, returns a reference to the new row.
table. insertCell: inserts a new col (<td>) in a given <tr>, returns a reference to the new col.

```
<style type="text/css">
  .tableClass{
    width:600px;
    border:1px solid #ff0000;
    border-collapse: collapse;
  }
  .tableClass td{
    border:1px solid #ff0000;
  }
</style>
```

```html
<input type="button" value="Create Table" onclick="doCreateTable()" />
<input type="button" value="Create Row" onclick="doCreateRow()" />
Rows:<input type="text" value="" id="row" /> Columns: <input type="text" value="" id="col" />
<br>
<br>
<div id="div">

</div>

<script type="text/javascript">
    var table;
    function doCreateTable()
    {
        table=document.createElement("table");
        table.className="tableClass";

        document.getElementById("div").appendChild(table);
    }

    function doCreateRow()
    {
        var rowNum=parseInt(document.getElementById("row").value);
        var colNum=parseInt(document.getElementById("col").value);

        for(var i=1;i<=rowNum;i++)
        {
            var row=table.insertRow(-1);
            for(var j=1;j<=colNum;j++)
            {
                var cell=row.insertCell(-1);
                cell.innerHTML="row: "+i+", col: "+j;
            }
        }
    }
</script>
```

Delete Table Row Column

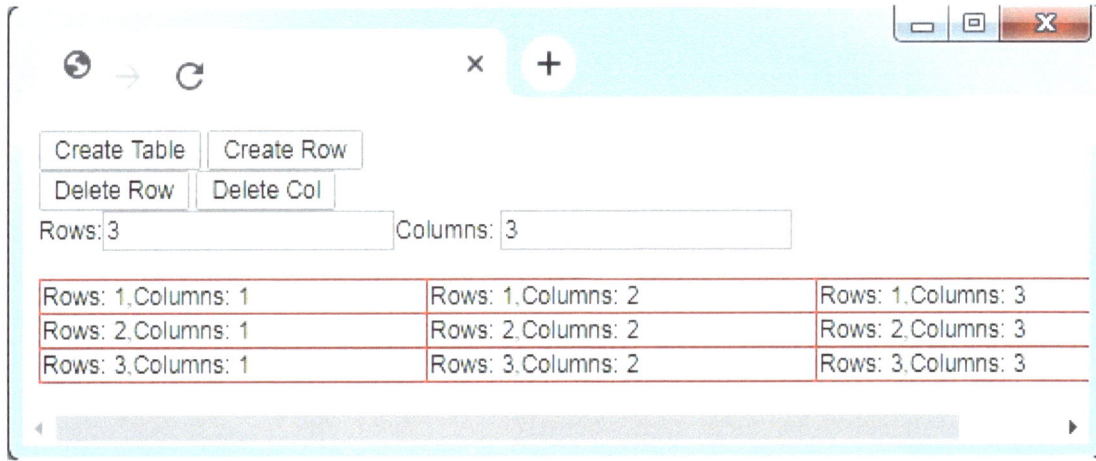

1. Create a DeleteTableRowColumn.html file with Notepad and open it in your browser

table. deleteCell: delete a cell in the current table row.

```html
<style type="text/css">
  .tableClass{
    width:600px;
    border:1px solid #ff0000;
    border-collapse: collapse;
  }

  .tableClass td{
    border:1px solid #ff0000;
  }
</style>
<input type="button" value="Create Table" onclick="doCreateTable()" />
<input type="button" value="Create Row" onclick="doCreateRow()" />
<br>
<input type="button" value="Delete Row" onclick="doDeleteRow()" />
<input type="button" value="Delete Col" onclick="doDeleteCol()" />
<br>
Rows:<input type="text" value="" id="row" />Columns: <input type="text" value="" id="col" />
<br>
<br>
<div id="div"> </div>
```

```html
<script type="text/javascript">
   var table;
   function doCreateTable()
   {
      table=document.createElement("table");
      table.className="tableClass";
      document.getElementById("div").appendChild(table);
   }

   function doCreateRow()
   {
      var rowNum=parseInt(document.getElementById("row").value);
      var colNum=parseInt(document.getElementById("col").value);

      for(var i=1;i<=rowNum;i++)
      {
         var row=table.insertRow(-1);
         for(var j=1;j<=colNum;j++)
         {
            var cell=row.insertCell(-1);
            cell.innerHTML="Rows: "+i+",Columns: "+j;
         }
      }
   }


   function doDeleteRow()
   {
      var rowNum=parseInt(document.getElementById("row").value);
      table.deleteRow(rowNum);
   }

   function doDeleteCol()
   {
      var colNum=parseInt(document.getElementById("col").value);
      var rows=table.rows;
      for(var i=0;i<rows.length;i++)
      {
         rows[i].deleteCell(colNum);
      }
   }
</script>
```

Timer

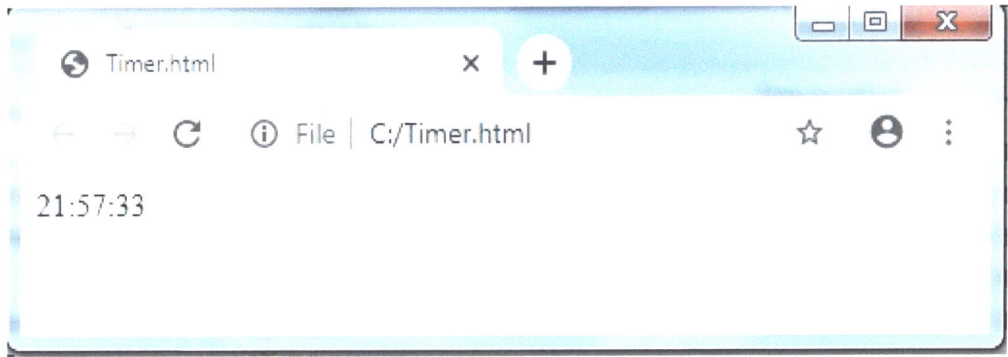

1. Create a Timer.html file with Notepad and open it in your browser

getFullYear(): Get the year as a four digit number (yyyy)
getMonth(): Get the month as a number (0-11)
getDate(): Get the day as a number (1-31)
getHours(): Get the hour (0-23)
getMinutes(): Get the minute (0-59)
getSeconds(): Get the second (0-59)
getTime(): Get the time (milliseconds since January 1, 1970)
setInterval(): continue calling the function until clearInterval() is called.

```
<div id="dateDiv" ></div>

<script type="text/javascript">
  function doSetInterval()
  {
     var dateDiv=document.getElementById("dateDiv");
     var d=new Date();
     var dateString = d.getHours()+":"+d.getMinutes()+":"+d.getSeconds()

     dateDiv.innerHTML=dateString;
  }

  setInterval("doSetInterval()",1000);
</script>
```

Thanks for learning, if you want to learn advance javascript, please study book

http://en.verejava.com

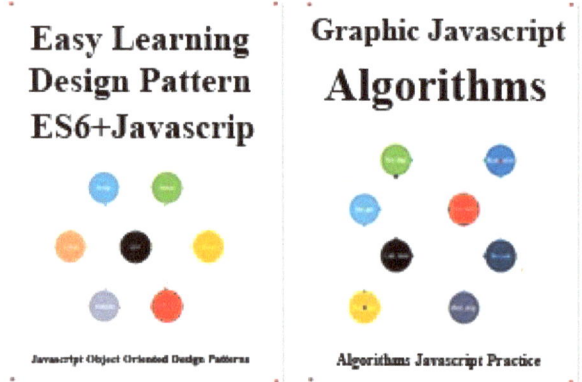

If you enjoyed this book and found some benefit in reading this, I'd like to hear from you and hope that you could take some time to post a review on Amazon. Your feedback and support will help us to greatly improve in future and make this book even better.

You can follow this link now.

http://www.amazon.com/review/create-review?&asin=B086PLBF4Z

Different country reviews only need to modify the amazon domain name in the link:
www.amazon.co.uk
www.amazon.de
www.amazon.fr
www.amazon.es
www.amazon.it
www.amazon.ca
www.amazon.nl
www.amazon.in
www.amazon.co.jp
www.amazon.com.br
www.amazon.com.mx
www.amazon.com.au

I wish you all the best in your future success!

www.ingramcontent.com/pod-product-compliance
Lightning Source LLC
Chambersburg PA
CBHW051913210526
45473CB00006B/1994